Three Creation Stories

Three Creation Stories

A Rabbi Encounters the Universe

MICHAEL GOLD

WIPF & STOCK · Eugene, Oregon

THREE CREATION STORIES
A Rabbi Encounters The Universe

Wipf & Stock
An Imprint of Wipf and Stock Publishers
199 W. 8th Ave., Suite 3
Eugene, OR 97401

www.wipfandstock.com

PAPERBACK ISBN: 978-1-5326-5375-9
HARDCOVER ISBN: 978-1-5326-5376-6
EBOOK ISBN: 978-1-5326-5377-3

Manufactured in the U.S.A.   10/29/18

To My Students

"Rabbi Hanina taught, Much have I learned from my teachers, more from my colleagues, but the most from my students." (*Talmud, Hagigah* 7a)

Contents

Diagrams

Acknowledgments

This book grew out of a conversation I had in 2011 with the head of my PhD dissertation committee, philosophy professor Marina P. Banchetti. I wanted to write a dissertation using the process philosophy of Alfred North Whitehead to interpret the creation story in the *Zohar*, the major work of Jewish mysticism. This would fulfill my department's requirements that the dissertation cover material in two academic disciplines—in my case philosophy and Jewish studies. At the time, I also wanted to add some material I had studied in the physics department about relativity and quantum physics. Professor Banchetti was clear: "Leave the science out. Put it in the book you will write after completing your dissertation."

Those words inspired this book. I want to thank the members of my dissertation committee: Professors Banchetti, Frederick E. Greenspahn, Kristen H. Lindbeck of Florida Atlantic University, and Professor Eitan P. Fishbane of the Jewish Theological Seminary of America. They were demanding in their expectations but encouraging in guiding me to develop my ideas about the role of mind in the universe.

While serving as a rabbi and working on my PhD, I also met in an attorney's office every Wednesday afternoon with a small study group. The class was titled "The Bible—and Everything Else Under the Sun." We spoke about everything, from creation to ethics to life after death. These discussions helped sharpen my thinking on the material covered in this book. Meanwhile, I was also teaching philosophy and religion at Broward College and Miami-Dade College. As I mentioned in the dedication, often I would learn as much from my students as from my textbooks.

I would like to thank the members of my congregation, Temple Beth Torah Sha'aray Tzedek in Tamarac, Florida, who allowed me to put philosophy and science into my many sermons and classes on Judaism. I want to thank my editor at Wipf & Stock, Matt Wimer, for believing in this book.

Last but not least, I want to thank my wife, Evelyn, for her infinite patience as I pursued multiple paths as rabbi, teacher, graduate student, professor, and writer—all at the same time. Without you I could never have done this.

Introduction—What Is Reality?

Three baseball umpires were discussing their profession. The first said, "Ball! Strike! I calls them as I sees them." The second said, "Ball! Strike! I calls them as they are." Finally, the third said, "Ball! Strike! They ain't nothing till I calls them."

A s a rabbi, I have always been fascinated by the fundamental question, What is reality? What is really out there? What is the universe made of, and how did it get here? Is the universe simply matter or is there a spiritual substance? What is the role of mind or soul or spirit in the universe? As humans, are we merely bodies? Or are we something more, spiritual beings? Are we material bodies or embodied spirits? If we are spiritual, what happens to that spirit when the body dies? Is there some kind of life after death and if so, what is it? How could a universe come from nothing? How can it go from the early chaos of the big bang to the organization of life, when by the laws of entropy everything should go from organization to chaos? If God created the universe, why is there evil? Does God change the laws of nature to create miracles? If we humans evolved from lower animals, why should we be ethical? Could we create a computer with a soul? Is nature alive and if so, should we worship nature? What is the light that God created on the first day? Did God create the universe, or did the universe emanate out of God? And finally, at the center of many of the discussions in this book, what is consciousness?

This book is an attempt to answer these questions. It will explore modern science, including some of the most contemporary areas of scientific thinking such as relativity, quantum theory, cosmology, evolution, and neuroscience. But it will also recognize the true limitations of science. There are questions that science cannot answer. This book will also move beyond science, into the broad area of philosophy known as metaphysics. The name *metaphysics* goes back to Aristotle, and his work that goes beyond physics. It deals with the question of reality. Is the universe made of two realities— mind and matter or body and spirit? This is the claim of dualists. Or is the universe made only of matter as materialists claim? Or perhaps the universe is made only of mind as idealists, Eastern religions, and many mystics claim. We will explore all three of these options.

Finally, we will look at religion, and in particular, the creation story at the beginning of Genesis. Based on Jewish tradition, we will look at three different interpretations of that creation story. One interpretation will take us toward dualism and a classical theistic view of God. This is the approach to religion with which I was raised, and the approach I taught during most of my early years as a rabbi. And yet this approach raises serious problems. A second interpretation will take us toward materialism, the view of the universe accepted by most modern scientists and philosophers. The universe is simply matter in motion, as Isaac Newton claimed. Yet this also raises serious problems, in particular, where does mind or consciousness come from in such a material universe.

We will also look at a third interpretation found amongst Jewish mystics. This will take us in a totally new direction, toward idealism and the view of mind and consciousness as the ultimate reality. If this is true, is everything part of one universal mind, as Hinduism teaches? Because we are exploring three interpretations of Genesis and three views of reality, I called this book *Three Creation Stories*. The book will be divided into three parts, the first part based on dualism, the second part based on materialism, and the third part based on idealism. But before we can begin, we must explore in greater depth the tools humans have used to understand reality: science, philosophy, and religion.

Science

When I began work on my PhD in the Public Intellectuals Program at Florida Atlantic University, I was encouraged to take courses in as broad a cross section of disciplines as possible. The university wanted public intellectuals to be well-rounded. Although I studied mostly philosophy, I also took such classes as Shakespeare in Film, European Politics, and Contemporary Social Theory. But my biggest challenge was a graduate seminar in Einstein's theory of general relativity.

I had been a mathematics major in college and thought I could handle it. On the first day, the professor said, "Go home and relearn calculus." In college I had tutored calculus, but I had not looked at it in over thirty years.

Luckily, it came back to me. And as I worked with the professor solving problems of gravitation and motion, space and time, I realized why I love science. Although I am a rabbi and not a scientist, I realize that any serious quest for reality must begin with science. I also realize that when there is a conflict between science and religion, as Maimonides taught in the twelfth century, the religion must be reinterpreted so that it does not conflict with the best scientific theories out there. So our quest must begin with science.

The story of the three umpires at the beginning of this chapter dates back to the early 1950s. Some say the story is even earlier; the words "they ain't nothing till I calls them" was said by a real umpire early in the twentieth century. Whatever the source of the story, the words point to a profound disagreement among scientists themselves. Does science simply describe a reality that is out there? Or do our minds create reality? Most of us believe the former. Yet I have seen quantum physicists use this umpire story to describe their scientific discipline. Our minds create reality through the act of observation. As we shall show, this is the thinking of many of the founders of quantum theory.

The beginning of the scientific revolution brought about by Copernicus, Kepler, Galileo, Newton, and Francis Bacon taught that there is a reality out there which we humans can comprehend. We do not learn about reality through philosophical speculation as taught by Aristotle and his scholastic interpreters such as Thomas Aquinas. It was time to throw out Aristotelian physics and come up with a new way of seeing the world. This would involve observation, measuring data, coming up with hypotheses, and using experiments to test those hypotheses. Out of this would grow scientific theories, often formulated in the language of mathematics. In fact, Galileo claimed that mathematics was the language God spoke. The underlying assumption was that our scientific theories described reality.

To these early thinkers of the scientific revolution, only science can give us a true picture of reality. There was no room for either metaphysics or religion in such a scientific world view. In the mid-twentieth century, a group of philosophers known as logical-positivists gathered in Vienna and held discussions that took this idea to an extreme. They claimed that there are two types of knowledge. One is simply knowledge that we know logically or by definition (e.g., $2 + 2 = 4$ or triangles have three sides). The other is scientific knowledge or what they called positive knowledge, anything that could be shown empirically. The earth travels around the sun or metals conduct electricity are positive knowledge. Everything else is mere speculation and, therefore, mere nonsense.

According to this Vienna Circle, we cannot talk about metaphysics or religion, God or ethics. Ludwig Wittgenstein (1889–1951), one of the leading thinkers of this movement, who many consider to be the greatest philosopher of the twentieth century, taught, "Whereof one cannot speak, thereof one must be silent." Part of Wittgenstein's greatness is that he later rejected this logical positivism for a new philosophy based totally on shared language. But to the early Wittgenstein, we can speak of logic and we can speak of science. Science is a true description of reality.

However, there is a problem with this description of science. From the beginning of the scientific revolution, some questioned the idea that science simply reflects reality. When Copernicus published his heliocentric view of the universe the day before his death, his publisher Andreas Osiander wrote a preface. In it he wrote that Copernicus is providing a nice mathematical model to predict the motions of heavenly bodies. But this mathematical work, although useful, does not reflect reality. Reality is actually the geocentric view of the universe reflected in the Bible. Of course, this statement was to pacify church authorities. Perhaps the lesson of Copernicus is that if one wants to challenge church dogma on science, like Copernicus one should publish on the day before one dies. Later Galileo, building on Copernicus's ideas, spent his final years under house arrest for challenging the church's view of the universe.

Copernicus's publisher challenges the popular view known as scientific realism, that science is a model of what is really out there. Scientific realism teaches that theories correspond to truths about the universe. If science predicts that certain events will cause certain other events, this reflects the true reality about the universe. Science tests its theories by looking for a correspondence between scientific theories and reality.

This view has been challenged by a second view, known as anti-realism or epistemic science. This teaches that science can only predict the results of experiments. No claims can be made about whether there is a reality corresponding to these results. The most obvious example of such epistemic science is quantum theory. Niels Bohr (1885–1962), one of the most important developers of the theory, taught that quantum theory is worthwhile because it accurately predicts results. In fact, this theory of the tiniest particles is one of the most accurate in the history of science. Yet, Bohr claims that quantum theory cannot tell us what is happening in reality. For example, at the quantum level an electron is not really a particle at all but rather a probability wave. By the Heisenberg uncertainty principle, we cannot pin down its location and its momentum at the same time. In fact, on the quantum level the behavior of what we call particles is extremely strange and impossible to pin down. Only when we run experiments do we come up with predictable results. We can know the results of our experiments, but we can never truly know reality.

Bohr and Einstein spent a lifetime arguing over whether quantum mechanics reflects an underlying reality or whether it is simply a good mathematical tool for making predictions on something unknowable. Historically, Bohr's epistemic view seems to have won out against Einstein's more realistic view. An epistemic view of science grows out of such contemporary scientific theories as quantum mechanics. Nonetheless, the roots of this approach lie with one of the greatest philosophers in human history, Immanuel Kant (1721–1804). Kant revolutionized how we think about the universe and our own minds, and we will return to his thought throughout this book. Kant considered his philosophy a Copernican revolution in how we see the universe. Just as Copernicus moved the center of the universe from the earth (geocentric) to the sun (heliocentric), so Kant moved how we see the universe.

Until Kant, philosophers believed they could come up with a God's eye view of the universe, how it really is in the eyes of God. Kant spoke about a turn to the subject. We can only know how the universe is by the way our mind organizes its view of the world. The human mind sees the world in terms of certain a priori categories of thought. Our mind organizes sense data so that we see the universe in a certain way. For example, until Kant people believed that space and time really exist as part of the universe, that God sees events happening in space and time. Kant said that we have no way of knowing if space and time really exist. We only know that our minds see the events in terms of space and time. Space and time are human constructions, not necessarily part of reality.

In fact, Kant said that all human beings can know about the world is what are mind perceives, what Kant called the phenomenal world. The world as it really is, what Kant called the "thing-in-itself" or the noumenal world, is totally unknowable. We humans can know what we see, hear, feel, taste, and smell, in other words, how our minds organize sense data. But reality is unknowable to the human mind. For Kant, the claim that reality is unknowable gave him room for religious faith. Kant said that he had to "limit human knowledge in order to make room for faith."

Human thinking from Kant to Bohr seems to point toward a nonrealistic view of science, that science can give us predictable results but we have no way of knowing if those results correspond to reality. Perhaps the greatest challenge to the idea that science gives us a true picture of reality belongs to recent philosophers of science Karl Popper and Thomas Kuhn. Both spoke of the limits of science. Let's briefly explore each of their thinking.

Popper (1902–1994), although influenced by the logical positivists mentioned above, realized that they are mistaken. Remember that logical positivists teach that there are only two kinds of true statements: logical statements and scientific statements. To be scientific, a statement must be verifiable. The test of truth is whether the statement can be verified. So to a logical positivist, "the earth travels around the sun" is true because it can be verified. "God exists" is not true because it cannot be verified. For the logical positivists, every statement must pass a verification test.

Popper taught that no statement can ever totally be verified. Statements can only be falsified. For example, scientists used to believe that "all swans are white." But there is no way to verify this statement without looking at every swan on earth. When people discovered a black swan in Australia, the statement was shown to be untrue. As a scientific statement, "all swans are white" was shown to be false. According to Popper, a statement is scientific if and only if it can be falsified.

The results are radical. Science can never give us truth. It can only give us probability. To be truly scientific, a statement must be falsifiable. Often people tell me, "Why am I religious? If I want to learn the answers, turn to science. Only science leads to truth." I love to answer, "Science can never lead to truth. True science, according to Popper, must be falsifiable. Some of the greatest theories of science, such as Newton's laws of gravitation, were eventually proven false by Einstein." This view that scientific theories are often falsified leads us to an even more radical view of science, that of historian Thomas Kuhn.

Kuhn (1922–1996) wrote a book titled *The Structure of Scientific Revolutions*, published in 1962. He claimed that most scientists, doing what he called normal science, work within a paradigm. But occasionally anomalies pop up that challenge that paradigm. For example, all physicists before Einstein worked in a Newtonian paradigm that time and space are fixed and objects move according to precise laws. But if that paradigm were true, the speed of light should vary depending on the movement of whoever is measuring it. In a famous experiment in 1887, Albert Michaelson and Edward Morley showed that the speed of light is always constant. This created an anomaly that challenged Newton, which no one could answer. It took Einstein almost thirty years later to develop his theory of special relativity, creating a new paradigm and overturning Newton.

Kuhn invented the phrase "paradigm shift." Scientists working in one paradigm have incommensurate differences with those working in another paradigm. This is what happened when Ptolemy's geocentric theory gave way to Copernicus's heliocentric theory. This is what happened when Lamarck's theory of biological change gave way to Darwin's theory of evolution. And this is what happened when Newtonian physics gave way to Einstein's theories of special and general relativity. According to Kuhn, scientific theories are never "true" but constantly open to shifts as new anomalies appear.

All of this indicates that as important as science is, it cannot give ultimate answers to reality. Just as Aristotle wrote a book called *Physics* and a book called *Metaphysics*, so we must carefully study science and then move beyond science. People often misuse the term "metaphysics" as part of the occult, tied in with crystals and tarot cards. But the actual meaning of metaphysics is the branch of philosophy that studies reality. Let us turn our attention to metaphysics to see if it can give us some answers to the question, what is really out there?

Philosophy

Besides being a full-time rabbi at a congregation, I also teach philosophy part time at two local community colleges. Occasionally my students challenge me. How can I see the world through both the eyes of faith as a clergy and the eyes of reason as a philosopher? It is a great question. After all, the church Father Tertullian famously said, "What has Athens to do with Jerusalem?" What does reason have to do with faith? And yet, some of the greatest thinkers in Jewish history combined religion with the philosophical quest. Saadia, Maimonides, Judah HaLevi, Martin Buber, Franz Rosenzweig, and Abraham Joshua Heschel all combined their religious faith with their philosophical writings. And one of the great medieval Christian philosophers, Anselm, the inventor of the ontological proof of God, called his philosophical work "faith seeking understanding." I hope this work will show that one can be fully religious and still remain part of that philosophical quest.

The earliest Greek philosophers were concerned with questions of the nature of reality. They believed that ultimate answers will not come from Greek myths about the gods or the great narratives by Homer. Rather, human reason can lead to ultimate truths. The first known pre- Socratic philosopher was Thales, who declared that water was the basis of everything. Anaximander taught that there was a primordial stuff called *apeiron*, which became differentiated into hot and cold, moist and dry. Anaximanes said air was the fundamental stuff. Pythagoras, impressed by the harmonies of the universe, said that numbers were the fundamental source of everything. All of these philosophers agreed that there was some fundamental substance underlying all of reality.

An additional argument amongst pre-Socratic philosophers was about the role of change in the universe. Parmenides claimed that since something cannot come from nothing, on a fundamental level nothing ever changes. Change is an illusion. One of his students, Zeno, came up with a series of paradoxes to prove that change is impossible. Heraclitus, on the other hand, taught that everything is in flux: "You cannot step into the same river twice." Plato tried to combine both these ideas by describing in his allegory of the cave, a constantly changing material reality with an unchanging World of the Forms. This World of the Forms is the ultimate reality. Plato's ideas will be vital later when we look at the human soul, an idea created by Plato and his teacher, Socrates. Empedocles spoke of a primary substance that divided into the four fundamental substances—earth, water, air, and fire. This would become a fundamental part of Aristotle's, a student of Plato's, view of reality.

Many of the Greeks were atomists, precursors of our modern materialists. Leucippus and his student Democritus taught that the world was made of tiny, indivisible particles. These particles collided together, forming everything that exists. In many ways, these Greeks foresaw the discovery of the atom long before microscopes existed. One can see from this that at the root of philosophy is an argument regarding the question, what is reality?

With modern philosophy, beginning with the French thinker René Descartes (1596–1650), a major debate regarding the nature of reality begins. The debate was over the nature of two substances: mind and matter or body and spirit. Descartes was a dualist, claiming that mind and matter both exist. Many thinkers such as Thomas Hobbes and Karl Marx were materialists, saying only one substance—matter—exists. Other thinkers such as George Berkeley and Georg Hegel were idealists, saying only one substance—mind—exists. The three-way argument is whether dualism (both mind and matter), materialism (just matter), or idealism (just mind) are the fundamental stuff of the universe. Each of our three creations stories will focus on one of these three approaches.

Descartes began his discourse with radical doubt. He doubted everything from religious tradition to the very existence of his own body. After all, perhaps an evil demon was creating the illusion that his body exists. (This is sometimes called "the brain in the vat" question. The movie *The Matrix* is a modern discussion of Descartes's thinking.) Finally, after eliminating everything else, Descartes found something he could not doubt. He could not doubt that he was doubting, he was thinking, he had a mind. He declared in Latin, *cogito ergo sum*: "I think therefore I am." Mind exists.

Descartes's next step was to prove God exists. Since he has a mind and since that mind has within it the concept of a perfect being, that concept must have come from somewhere. Therefore, the perfect being must exist. This is a version of the ontological proof of God, going from the idea of God in the mind to the reality of God out there. Finally, Descartes concluded that since God exists, God would not deliberately fool him into thinking he has a body. He was not a mind in a vat. His body must really exist. Since he has proven that he has both a mind and a body, using two different proofs, Descartes concluded that they are two different substances—mind and body. Descartes was a dualist.

Of course, there are problems with Descartes's analysis. First, Descartes was a dualist only regarding human beings. His Christian faith led him to the belief that humans have a body and a soul. But animals are merely bodies, automatons without a mind. Even in his own time Descartes was attacked for this idea. Most of us believe our pet dogs and cats have a mind. But it is a profound religious question whether our pets have souls.

The bigger question for Descartes, and for all dualists, is: how do the body and the mind interact? It is obvious that they must interact. My mind chooses to walk somewhere, and my body follows. Give my body certain substances, like half a bottle of vodka, and my mind is affected. How can two different substances affect one another? Descartes tried to respond by saying that the interaction takes place in the pineal gland. Today we know this is not true. But the biggest problem for dualism is, how can two different substances like body and mind interact with each other?

Despite this problem, most of us who live in the West and who had any kind of traditional religious upbringing are dualists. We have a body and a soul. We are the product of Plato, with his vision of the imperfect changing material world and the perfect unchanging World of the Forms. Our soul comes from this perfect World of the Forms only to return there when we die. The belief that we have a body and a soul, and when we die our body returns to the dust but our soul returns to God, is pure dualism. It is the effect of Plato on Western religion, through the interpretation of Augustine of Hippo. Augustine's project was to combine the Bible with Plato, creating such a dualism. Most scholars argue that such a dualism, the separation of the body and soul, was not part of the original Bible. Religion borrowed it from the Greeks.

Today dualism has fallen out of favor with most modern thinkers, both scientists and philosophers. They question the presence of a substance like mind or soul that is totally separate from matter, but which can influence matter. How can something that is outside the material world cause movement within the material world? Does this not break with the laws of conservation of motion? As we will show in a future chapter, some of these philosophers will try to explain mind or consciousness in purely material terms.

Such scientists and philosophers are materialists, saying that everything is matter. Some use the phrase "materialistic monists." Monism means there is one substance and the claim that it is material. Others use the term "physicalism." Everything that exists can be explained by the laws of physics. The entire universe is bits of matter moving by natural laws in time and space. As we showed above, the ancient Greek atomists such as Leucippus and his student Democritus already taught this idea. They are the original materialist thinkers. But modern materialism has its roots in the medieval philosopher William of Ockham (1287–1347).

Ockham taught a theory that came to be known as Ockham's razor. One should not multiply entities beyond what is necessary to explain phenomena. Ockham was hardly a modern materialist. He was reacting to the Platonic idea of the forms and other spiritual entities. With Ockham, there were only the material entities that we can perceive in the world. Philosophers used the term "nominalism" to explain his philosophy, from a word meaning "to name." What Plato called the forms are simply names we give to certain object. Modern philosophers would use Ockham's razor to cut away the presence of any spiritual substances. A single substance, the material, is sufficient to explain the world.

Perhaps the first modern philosopher to develop a materialist understanding of reality was Thomas Hobbes (1588–1679). The universe was merely matter in motion. Human beings too were matter in motion. That is why Hobbes saw humans as fundamentally selfish and violent, and life in the world was "solitary, poor, nasty, brutish, and short." Only a very strong government, which Hobbes called the Leviathan, named after the biblical sea creature, can keep humans in line.

Other Enlightenment thinkers, trusting in the scientific revolution and skeptical of religion, would continue the material tradition. The French cosmologist Pierre-Simon Laplace (1749–1827) famously taught that if a being with superior intelligence knew the location and momentum of every particle in the universe, such a being could predict the entire future and retrodict the entire past. The world is made of pieces of matter that move according to predictable scientific laws. Everything is predetermined. (Of course, modern quantum theory, with its use of randomness and statistics, challenged this clock-work universe. This always bothered Einstein, who said that "the Old One does not play dice with the universe.")

Numerous other thinkers continued down this materialist line. Karl Marx (1818–1883) was a materialist who said that economic forces alone determine the entire future. Sigmund Freud (1856–1939) was also a materialist who said that certain unconscious drives, particularly the sexual and aggressive drive, determine all human behavior. Both Marx and Freud would deny the presence of a free will, a mind separate from the material and able to make free choices.

Where does God fit into this materialistic vision? Many early Enlightenment thinkers moved away from a God who intervenes in the universe (theism) toward a God who set the matter in motion but does not intervene (deism). To deists, God may have created a world but since then the world runs by natural laws. God neither answers prayers nor performs miracles. In fact, one of the most prominent deists of the Enlightenment, Thomas Jefferson (1743–1826), who wrote the American Declaration of Independence, prepared a Bible where he removed all mention of God's miracles. Copies of this "Jefferson Bible" still exist today.

Materialism may fit in with Ockham's razor, removing unnecessary entities. But it also creates a difficult question. Where does consciousness fit in? Could matter in motion have a mind, think and feel? Could we build a computer with a sense of self-identity, that says "I exist"? We will explore all these options. But to many thinkers, picturing a reality made of matter only without mind is extremely problematic. Many would prefer to follow the path of the Eastern religions such as Hinduism and Western mystics, saying that not only is mind part of reality, mind is the ultimate reality.

A third approach to the question of reality is idealism, or as some call it, idealistic monism. There is only one reality and that is mind. Mind permeates everything. Or as ancient Hindu tradition teaches, *Atman* is *Brahman* ("each individual soul is part of the universal mind"). Everything is part of that universal consciousness. In China, similar ideas developed in Daoism, the idea that there is a universal reality which flows, and humans must live their lives in keeping with that reality.

In the West, the first to develop a truly idealist view of reality was Plotinus (204–270). He was the major interpreter of Plato, who had great influence on later thinkers, particularly mystics of various faiths. His philosophy is Neoplatonism. He taught that the material world flowed out of a universal mind, much as a brook flows out of a spring. This mind is part of all reality, and the goal of each individual soul is to reunite with that universal reality. The soul needs to return to God. Jewish, Christian, and Muslim mystics all developed their interpretations of the world on Plotinus's ideas.

The first Western philosopher to introduce idealism was George Berkeley (1685–1753). It was Berkeley who raised the question, if a tree falls in a forest and nobody is there to hear it, does it make a sound? The answer is no, for a sound is something someone hears. If there is nobody to hear, then there is no sound. Berkeley would probably answer that God does perceive it. In fact, this is the idealist proof of God—if to exist is to be perceived, there must be something around to perceive everything. To this idealist, God is the ultimate mind.

Idealism often gets short shrift in philosophy textbooks. I teach philosophy at a local college and my textbook speaks at length about dualism and materialism, but it almost dismisses idealism. But particularly in this time of new sciences including relativity and quantum theory, where perception is central, it is worth giving idealism reconsideration.

Earlier in this introduction we already mentioned Kant. In a sense, Kant was an idealist. He did not deny the existence of a real world out there, the noumenal world, but he claimed that human beings can never know it. The term often used for Kant's philosophy is "transcendental idealism." The term *transcendental* implies the presence of a subject or human mind at the center of perception. Kant's view is often called "the turn to the subject."

Georg Wilhelm Friedrich Hegel (1770–1831) was the most influential philosopher of the nineteenth century. He built on the idealism of Kant (and other idealists such as Schopenhauer) to build a philosophy of everything based on mind. Mind, or what Hegel called *geist*, is dynamic, constantly evolving. It goes through a series of stages that Hegel called the dialectic, which included the thesis, the antithesis, and then the synthesis. All of human history is this dialectic of mind. (Later Marx would take Hegel's ideas, stand them on their head, and build a materialistic dialectic based not on mind but on economics.) Some have said that mystical thinking such as Kabbalah influenced Hegel, and that the mystical presence of God goes through this same dialectic.

Contemporary science was certainly influenced by these idealistic thinkers. In fact, before Einstein came up with his theory of special relativity, he studied Kant. In special relativity, mind and the observer become important. Time and space will vary depending on who is doing the measuring. A person standing still and a person travelling past at half the speed of light will measure time and space differently.

Relativity may depend on the observer. But with the quantum theory of the atom, the observer becomes central. Until an observer measures an object, it has no reality. It is simply a probability wave. Or as Schrodinger put it with his cat paradox, a cat can be in a box with a fifty-fifty chance that a certain quantum event will happen. An atom will decay releasing poison or the atom will not decay and not release poison. But until someone observes it, the cat is both alive and dead at the same time. Observation creates reality.

Where is God in this idealistic view of reality? If mind is everything, then God is the ultimate mind. God is the consciousness of the universe. This is the reason why many writers have seen parallels between Eastern mysticism and quantum theory. We will explore these ideas further.

So, which of these approaches is a more accurate view of reality? Are the dualists like Plato and Descartes correct? Are the materialists like Hobbes and Laplace correct? Or are the idealists like Berkeley and Kant correct? We seem to be no closer than when we started to an answer to the question, what is reality? Perhaps this is the time to turn to religion, which claims to give answers to unanswered questions.

Religion

If we are going to search for ultimate answers, we must turn to the discipline that asks ultimate questions. Almost every religion has some kind of narrative about where the world came from and why we are here. For me, as a Jew and a rabbi, that means turning to my own tradition, written in the Torah or the Five Books of Moses. In particular, it means looking at the creation story at the beginning of Genesis.

Jews have never been biblical literalists. From the beginning Jews have recognized that these words are open to interpretation. In fact, the greatest Jewish biblical commentator, Rashi (1040–1105), remarks about the beginning of Genesis, "This verse cries out, interpret me." Later in this book we point to some of the grammatical problems with this chapter that require such interpretation. For the moment, let me simply say that I believe Genesis chapter 1 contains profound religious lessons about living in the world, but is not literally true.

The ancient Greeks taught that there are two forms of truth: logos and mythos. Logos is logical, empirical, scientific truth, the kind of truth we learn rationally. Mythos, on the other hand, is truth that may not be literally true but that teaches us about realities in the universe. A myth may come in the form of a story or narrative, or may be tied to an ancient ritual. We learn mythos from our parents and grandparents, from our community, sitting around a campfire looking at the stars. Is mythos true? One can equally ask, are Aesop's fables true? They may not be literally true, but they reflect profound truths about the universe.

Religious truth is mythos rather than logos. Nobody but the most extreme biblical literalists turn to the creation story in Genesis, written millennia ago, to learn scientific truth. To deny evolution because it does not match the biblical creation story, because the Bible speaks of species created in their entirety, is to misread what the creation story is all about. The Bible is mythos. Its purpose is to teach us lessons about what it means to be a human. We will explore in great detail throughout this book some of these lessons about being human. But if we become fixated on reading the Bible literally, we will immediately run into trouble. For example, God says on the first day, "there was evening there was morning, one day." But the sun and moon were not created until the fourth day, so obviously there was not a real night and day. Later we will learn what I believe these words really mean.

As a rabbi searching for reality, my starting place must be the creation story in Genesis. But I must read that document the way rabbinic tradition has read it for thousands of years. It is not and never was a literal description of reality. Rather, it is a document open to interpretation. In fact, the rabbis teach that there is never a fixed meaning of any Jewish text including the Torah itself. Jewish tradition says that there are multiple ways to read every text, all of them legitimate. In a sense, the Jewish approach is similar to the Catholic approach, which has a long history of ongoing interpretation of texts. This is at variance with the Protestant approach, of Luther's comment of *sola scriptura*; the text has a fixed meaning, which is the only authority. The rabbis say, on the contrary, that every word of Torah has seventy different meanings.[1]

The rabbis taught that there are four ways to read every scriptural text. (The Catholic Church has a similar four-fold theory of interpretation.) On the basic level, there is the *peshat* or literal meaning. What did it mean to whoever wrote it? The Talmud does say that a text never leaves its literal meaning.[2] But this is only the beginning of interpretation. There is *derash* (literally "searching") where a text is compared to other texts throughout the biblical canon to learn insights and meanings. An entire library of Jewish learning known as *midrash* is based on the use of *derash*. Third, there is *remez*, literally "hint." This is the use of allegory, often of a philosophical nature, and other insights to give meaning to the text. So, for example, the Alexandrian Jewish philosopher Philo (25 BCE—50 CE) saw the Torah as an allegory of the Platonic journey of the soul into the body.

Finally, there is an entire mystical tradition of interpretation known as *sod*, or "secret." Verses are interpreted not only for their meaning, but for the shapes and sounds of letters. Often *sod* uses *gematria*, a Hebrew numerology that gives each letter a numerical value. A vast Jewish mystical literature, including the *Zohar*, written in thirteenth-century Spain but attributed to a second-century rabbi, is a mystical interpretation of the Torah. I wrote my PhD dissertation on the creation chapters of the *Zohar* and will share some of my insights later in this book. Putting these four Hebrew terms together, *peshat, remez, derash, sod* spells out the Hebrew word *pardes* or "orchard." We get the English word "paradise" from this term.

---

1. See, for example, *Numbers Rabbah* 13:15.
2. See *Babylonian Talmud Shabbat* 63a among other sources.

The name for the branch of philosophy that studies interpretations of texts, particularly biblical interpretation, is called hermeneutics. Hermeneutics has a long history. Early scholars of hermeneutics, such as the Christian theologian Friedrich Schleiermacher (1768–1834), taught that scripture has a fixed meaning that the interpreter seeks to uncover. As mentioned above, this is close to Martin Luther's Protestant understanding of scripture. The major philosopher of hermeneutics from the twentieth century, Hans-Georg Gadamer (1900–2002), taught that there is no such thing as a God's eye view of the text; the interpreter stands within a particular community. Gadamer spoke of a "fusion of horizons," bringing together the meaning of a text with the needs of a community. In a sense, Gadamer is reflecting ideas we already presented about Kant. Kant taught that there is no God's eye view of the universe; Gadamer taught that there is no God's eye view of a text.

In my own thinking, I was influenced by a far more radical philosopher of interpretation, the founder of deconstruction Jacques Derrida (1930–2004) taught that "the text stands alone"—there is no fixed meaning to any text. Scriptural texts invite open-ended interpretation. Derrida was a Jew who claimed to be an atheist, although I see him as much more of a mystic. Derrida's approach to texts, according to religious scholar Karen Armstrong, is "positively rabbinical." Like Derrida, the rabbis over the generations have seen the texts of Judaism as open ended, allowing a variety of interpretations.

In this book we will be presenting three very different interpretations of the first few verses of Genesis. That will be the basis of the three creation stories that are at the heart of this book. The first creation story will take us toward dualism and classical theism, the way most Jews as well as Christians and Muslims understand their religion. The second creation story will take us toward materialism and deism, the way Enlightenment figures understood God's relation to the world. The third creation story will take us toward idealism and mysticism, a more radical view of reality. Hopefully, in exploring three different creations stories and three views of God and reality, we can begin to answer the fundamental question I have asked my entire life: what is really out there?

PART I

The First Creation Story—Dualism

א בְּרֵאשִׁית בָּרָא אֱלֹהִים אֵת הַשָּׁמַיִם וְאֵת הָאָרֶץ׃ ב וְהָאָרֶץ הָיְתָה תֹהוּ וָבֹהוּ וְחֹשֶׁךְ עַל־פְּנֵי תְהוֹם וְרוּחַ אֱלֹהִים מְרַחֶפֶת עַל־פְּנֵי הַמָּיִם׃ ג וַיֹּאמֶר אֱלֹהִים יְהִי־אוֹר וַיְהִי־אוֹר׃ ד וַיַּרְא אֱלֹהִים אֶת־הָאוֹר כִּי־טוֹב וַיַּבְדֵּל אֱלֹהִים בֵּין הָאוֹר וּבֵין הַחֹשֶׁךְ׃ ה וַיִּקְרָא אֱלֹהִים לָאוֹר יוֹם וְלַחֹשֶׁךְ קָרָא לָיְלָה וַיְהִי־עֶרֶב וַיְהִי־בֹקֶר יוֹם אֶחָד׃

"In the beginning God created the heaven and the earth. And the earth was without form, and void; and darkness was upon the face of the deep. And the Spirit of God moved upon the face of the waters. And God said, Let there be light: and there was light. And God saw the light, that it was good: and God divided the light from the darkness. And God called the light Day, and the darkness he called Night. And the evening and the morning were the first day."

(Genesis 1:1–5)

CHAPTER 1

Theism—Can We Still Believe?

The Talmud tells the story of the Roman emperor Antonius who said to the rabbi, "the body and the soul can both release themselves from judgment. The body can plead, the soul made me sin for since it left me I lie here like a dumb stone. The soul can plead, the body made me sin for since it left me I fly around like a bird." The rabbi replied, "I will tell you a parable. To what can it be compared? To a human king with a beautiful orchard growing splendid figs. Now there were two watchmen, one lame and one blind. One day the lame man climbed on the back of the blind man and the two of them stole some figs. The owner of the orchard confronted them. What became of my beautiful figs? The lame man said, 'do I have feet to walk with?' The blind man said, 'do I have eyes to see with?' What did the owner do? He put the blind man and the lame man together for judgment. So the Holy One Blessed be He puts the body and the soul together and judges them."[1]

I teach an Introduction to Philosophy class at the local community college. At the first class I always introduce my students to the ancient Greeks. My students are mostly young, freshmen and sophomores, and mostly from Christian backgrounds. A few are older, later in life students. I always ask them, "Have any of you ever heard the idea that we live in a world filled with decay and corruption? But, do not worry. One day our soul will depart this

---

1. *Babylonian Talmud Sanhedrin 91a–b.*

world and return to the perfect place from whence it came. Who taught you that?" They tell me they heard it from their priest, minister, or pastor; some say their rabbi or imam. I then shock them when I respond, "What if I told you that these ideas are not in the Bible. What you have heard is pure Plato. Western religions borrowed this from the Greeks."

The God of Theism

Our first creation story is the one most of us in the West grew up with. It is the religion of Jews, Christians, and Muslims (as opposed to Eastern religions like Hinduism and Buddhism). This creation story is based on the King James translation of the Bible of 1611, also known as the Authorized Version. In this translation, we see an all-powerful God creating an entire universe from absolute nothingness. This approach to religion goes by the name classical theism. Most Jews, Christians, and Muslims who take their religion seriously are classical theists.

To create the entire heaven and earth from absolute nothingness defies the old Greek notion, mentioned by Parmenides, that to create something from nothing is impossible. The Greeks believed that there was no particular moment in time when the world was created. Aristotle taught that universe has always existed. Unlike the Greeks, the Bible seems to teach that on the contrary, God at a certain moment in time created the universe by an act of pure will from absolute nothingness. The Latin term for such creation from nothing is *creation ex nihilo*. Many classical biblical commentators and most modern biblical scholars will question whether such *creation ex nihilo* was the intention of the biblical author. But this certainly seems to be the intention of the King James translation. One moment there was nothing and then in the next moment an entire universe came into being through an act of divine will.

This theistic view of creation also teaches that God used divine speech to create a universe. "God said, Let there be light: and there was light." The first chapter of Genesis continues with each step of creation. Each morning religious Jews, when they begin their preliminary morning prayers, say a prayer that begins with the words, "Blessed is He Who spoke and the world came into being." The power of words is a major theme throughout biblical literature. Christians in the Gospel of John teach, "In the beginning was the word, and the word was with God, and the word was God" (John 1:1). The Greek word for "word" is *logos*, a word we use today to mean rational thought. With rational thought and the use of words, God created an entire universe.

What are we saying about God by the claim that God created the universe through an act of speech out of nothing? Perhaps the most important idea is that God is all-powerful. Or to use the term of classical theism, God is omnipotent. God can do anything that it is possible to do. (Using the term "possible" removes all the rather nutty paradoxes of medieval scholastics such as, can God create a stone He cannot lift?) God has the maximum power possible for any being to have.

The theistic view also views God as possessing all knowledge, of knowing everything. Here we use the term omniscient. God knows everything there is to know about the universe He created. (I will use the term "he" for the moment because classical theism paints a rather masculine image of God. Many modern thinkers have rethought their image of God, using more feminine terms. More about this when we speak of mysticism later in this book.) Of course, if God knows everything, there are some difficult paradoxes. For example, does God know the future? Does God know what I will do tomorrow? If the answer is "yes," as most theists claim, then how can I have free will? If God knows that I will have Cheerios for breakfast tomorrow, am I making a free choice when I decide to eat Cheerios? The book of Exodus teaches that God knew in advance that Pharaoh would harden his heart, so was Pharaoh acting freely? If not, why did God punish Pharaoh?

Theists have come up with answers. For example, they say that God lives outside time, and therefore sees the past, present, and future all at once. But we humans live within time, remembering the past, living in the present, and making choices about the future. Therefore, from our perspective we have free will. From God's perspective everything has already been decided. It is like a movie, where God has the entire movie reel in front of Him and knows the ending, but the characters in the movie feel like they are acting freely. This answer is tied into the nature of time, a very complex question that we will explore later when we consider relativity.

Theists believe that God is omnipresent. God is everywhere at once. If God created all of space, then God can be found in all of space. This is the basis of one of the great Hasidic teachings Menachim Mendel of Kostz taught, "Where is God? Wherever we let Him in." Of course, this lovely teaching seems to indicate that until we let him in, God is not yet there. That point becomes very important in Jewish mystical and Hasidic teaching.

Finally, theists believe that God is all good. Some use the term benevolent or omnibenevolent. If God is good, then everything God does must be for the good. The prophet Isaiah already challenges this idea. He describes a God who "forms light and creates darkness, makes peace and creates evil" (Isaiah 45:7). The answer given by many theists to this verse from Isaiah is that what seems to be evil in our eyes is actually good in the eyes of God.

For goodness, by definition, is whatever God does. From this point of view, there is no evil in the world because from God's perspective, everything is good. We will devote an entire chapter to this question.

So we have a vision of God who is omniscient, omnipotent, omnipresent, omnibenevolent, perfect in every way. Anselm, who we mentioned in the introduction, used these various perfections to prove God's existence. According to Anselm, we have the ability in our minds to imagine a perfect being. This being would contain every perfection mentioned above. Is it closer to perfection to exist or not to exist? Anselm claims that it is closer to perfection to exist, and therefore this perfect being must exist. This is called the ontological proof of God. (Ontological means "being"; this is a proof from the being or the very definition of God.) Descartes used a version of this proof to prove that God exists.

Now we are ready to describe Western religions as they have historically been understood. An all-powerful God created a world from nothing. God set the laws of this world he created into motion. Now and again God, being all-powerful, can set aside some of those laws. For example, God can make the sea part, allowing the Israelites to cross over and then drown the Egyptians in the sea. God can cause the sun to stand still for Joshua. From a Christian perspective, God can even resurrect Jesus from the dead. We will dedicate a chapter to the question of miracles.

God through a revelation in Holy Scriptures can make his will known to human beings. God can give the Ten Commandments to the entire people Israel at Mt. Sinai. God becomes the source of right and wrong, and ethics means living in accordance with God's will. Ethics becomes simply obeying God and the unethical becomes disobeying God. We will also devote a chapter to ethics.

This is a God worthy of our prayers. God can hear our prayers and sometimes answer them. He can perform miracles on our behalf, bringing about healing. When we die, God can reward us or punish us according to our deeds. This is a God not only of this world but of the world-to-come. This is also a God who will send a redeemer in the end of days, what Jews call the Messiah or "anointed one," ushering an age of peace. Finally, everything that happens in this world is the result of God's will. As the midrash teaches, "Every blade of grass has an angel that bends over it and whispers, grow!"[2]

If everything happens by the will of God, then Jews say regularly *Be-yertze Hashem*—"By the will of God." Similarly, Muslims say *Insha'Allah*—"If Allah wills it." Christians can sing that old American spiritual, "He's got

2. *Bereishit Rabbah* 10:6.

the whole world in his hands." But if God is all-powerful and controls everything, what does that say about the world God created?

God's Creation

The first chapter of Genesis teaches that God created the heaven and the earth by a singular act of divine will. Then the Torah goes on to fill in a series of steps in this creation. On the first day God creates the light, separating the light and the darkness. On the second day God separates the upper waters from the lower waters. In biblical times people believed that the world was set between upper waters above the sky and lower waters under the ground. When God brought the great flood in the time of Noah, he opened up the gateway to these upper waters, allowing the upper and lower waters to mingle once again.

On the third day God creates the plants—trees, grasses, and vegetables. On the fourth day God creates the sun, moon, and the stars. Of course, how could there be evening and morning without a sun? This is clear proof that this story is meant as mythos and not a literal description of reality. On the fifth day God creates the lower animals—the insects, fish, birds, and swarming things. On the sixth day God creates the higher animals, such as mammals. And finally, toward the end of the sixth day God creates humanity.

The world was created step-by-step, leading from lower to higher forms of life. It is easy to fit the theory of the evolution of life through stages into this poetic vision. It is clear that the six days of creation could not be literal days. One can see the days as periods of time. After all, the Bible does teach that "For a thousand years in Thy sight are but as yesterday when it is past, as a watch in the night" (Psalms 90:4). We cannot judge time in the eyes of God as we judge time in the eyes of humanity. (Einstein will prove that time is never fixed but depends on the observer. Different observers will measure time differently. Could Einstein's laws of relativity explain the six days of creation from God's perspective?)

Finally, it is clear that humanity is qualitatively different from the rest of God's creation. Only humans are created in the image of God. Only humans can rule over the rest of the animal kingdom. Humans have a special ontological status different from the rest of creation. This was the basis of Descartes's belief mentioned in the introduction that only humans have souls, that animals are mere automatons.

Studying this vision of creation, we find a created universe that is passive, set in motion by an all-powerful God and moving according to natural laws. Perhaps now and again God interrupts these natural laws to perform a miracle. But in general, the universe presents a regularity that allows science to flourish. Scientists can study how these God-created laws work.

What is the nature of this universe that God created? Let us take a moment and look at three different answers to that question. The first is the classical view throughout the Middle Ages, articulated by Aristotle and favored by the Muslim thinker Averroes (1126–1198), the Jewish thinker Maimonides (1135–1204), and the Christian thinker Thomas Aquinas (1225–1274). Each thinker tried to combine their particularly religious faith with the works of Aristotle. The second is the Hermetic mystical tradition, which gave an occult vision of the universe and became extremely influential during the early Renaissance period. Finally, the third is the scientific revolution mechanical universe understandable through mathematics.

Each of these three approaches will be important as we develop our ideas throughout this book. Each confronted the other two in what Renaissance scholar Jeffrey Easlea called a "three cornered contest." To quote Easlea, "Modern science emerged, at least in part, out of a three-cornered contest between proponents of the established view and adherents of newly prospering magical cosmologies, both to be opposed in the seventeenth century advocates of revived mechanical world views. Scholastic Aristotelianism versus magic versus mechanical philosophies!"[3] Let us try to describe each of these three points of view.

Throughout the Middle Ages, Aristotle's thought became the accepted view of reality. It is worthy to give a summary of Aristotle's cosmology. To understand Aristotle we need to contrast him with his teacher, Plato. Plato believed that this material world was a pale imitation of another more spiritual world, what Plato called the World of the Forms. There was a spiritual reality that could be reached through our mind that was the true reality. The material world was a place of change and decay. For example, an individual horse in this world was a poor imitation of the form of a horse, which existed only in the spiritual World of the Forms. The goal of philosophers was to leave this material world, at least within our mind, and enter the perfect World of the Forms. Plato articulated this vision in his famous allegory of the cave, where the material world were mere shadows on a wall. The true philosopher can see the light above that is casting those shadows.

Aristotle was Plato's student who rejected the view of his teacher; he developed his view of the world in reaction to Plato. He rejected this World of the Forms. There was only this world, available through the senses. Aristotle was the forerunner of later empiricism, which taught that "there is

3. Easlea, *Witch Hunting*, 89.

nothing in the mind which is not first in the senses." There is no form of a horse, only individual horses. Form cannot exist without matter. With every substance in the world we can study four causes. There is the material cause, what it is made of. There is the formal cause, how it is formed. There is the efficient cause, how it came to be, the kind of things scientists would study.

For Aristotle, the key point is the fourth cause, what he called the final cause or purpose. Everything has a final cause or purpose, what philosophers call a teleology. And all motion on earth is caused by substances seeking to fulfill their cause or purpose. I love teaching Aristotle to my philosophy students. I ask them to point out each of the causes—material, formal, efficient, and final—for various objects. What are the four causes of a statue? (The material cause may be marble or stone, the formal cause is the shape, the efficient cause is a sculptor made it, and the final cause is the purpose the sculptor had in mind—for example, to commemorate a war hero.) I will ask the four causes of a boat, a tree, and a human being. (When I ask the final cause of a tree, I get some fascinating answers. The purpose of a tree is to provide shade, to prevent erosion, to provide fruit, to provide wood. The more sophisticated students say that trees are here to provide oxygen so mammals can exist. I tell them that they are being extremely anthropocentric. Is it true that trees were created for the sake of people? We will explore this further in the chapter on nature.)

The key idea of Aristotle is that everything has its place and everything has its purpose. The earth is at the center, and the sun and planets move around in a perfect circle fulfilling their purpose. Stones fall to the earth because they are seeking their place. Fire moves upward seeking its place. Even humans have a purpose, to be rational animals. Aristotle built an entire ethical system, often called virtue ethics, on humans seeking to fulfill their divine purpose. We can see now why Aristotle fit in so nicely with such religious thinkers as Averroes, Maimonides, and Aquinas. If everything has a purpose and a final cause, God must be the source of that final cause. All movement in the universe is simply substances seeking to fulfill God's purpose. Teleology fills the universe.

As we will show, modern science totally rejects Aristotle's picture of the universe. The idea of any divine cause or purpose behind the movement of matter is unacceptable. The Nobel Laureate Steven Weinberg in his book *The First Three Minutes* famously wrote, "The more the universe seems comprehensible, the more it also seems pointless."[4] Aristotle's idea of final causation was already under challenge during the Renaissance period. But

---

4. Weinberg, *First Three Minutes*, 154.

an alternative was also present, much closer to Plato, which spoke of spiritual or occult forces, often called the Hermetic view of the universe.

Hermetic teachings have their roots in ancient wisdom literature, reaching back to a prophet from ancient Egypt named Hermes, often called Hermes Trismegistus (Hermes the thrice great). It is the basis of a number of occult and magical traditions, an image of a universe filled with sympathies and antipathies that creates motion. Mind permeated much of creation. Some would say that the world was enchanted. Philosophical approaches such as Gnosticism and Neoplatonism also pictured a world filled with spiritual realities. We will explore these approaches shortly.

Such human activities as alchemy and astrology could allow humans to connect and influence these occult powers and spiritual realities. Various mystical traditions such as kabbalah also influenced many who followed these Hermetic traditions. In fact, Christian cabbala (their spelling) became a major area of study for such thinkers as Marsilio Ficino (1433–1499) and Giordano Bruno (1548–1600). Bruno was burned at the stake by the church for many of these ideas, including the idea that the world is infinite.

Many scholars see this Hermetic tradition as the true beginning of the scientific revolution.[5] In particular, these occult traditions emphasized the ability of human beings to manipulate creation and affect these various sympathies and empathies. In fact, these ideas greatly influenced Isaac Newton when he developed his theory of gravity. Gravity must be an occult force, if one body can affect another body across space, such as the sun pulling on the earth. Newton's writings were not simply scientific but filled with occult speculations.

These ideas saw the return of Platonic ideas to the world, which saw the presence of spiritual entities permeating the universe. One approach was known as Gnosticism which taught that there is secret knowledge (gnosis) to help the soul return to its spiritual source. Gnostic thinking was common in the early centuries of the common area. In fact, an entire library of gnostic manuscripts was found was found at Nag Hammadi in Egypt in 1945. Most of these manuscripts taught the idea that the created world is a place tinged with evil, and the goal of the soul was to escape to a more spiritual world. Early Christians considered this a heresy because it did not emphasize the role of Christ in the soul's search for salvation. But gnostic literature was extremely influential in later mystical writings.

5. For example, see Yates, *Giordano Bruno*.

Perhaps more important for later influence was the pagan interpreter of Plato's ideas Plotinus, the founder of what is called Neoplatonism. To Plotinus the ultimate reality was not an all-powerful God creating a passive world. Rather God literally flowed into the world much like a spring that becomes a mountain brook. The world is filled with God's presence. The human soul is literally part of this God that flowed into the world, and the goal of the soul should be to return to the place it came from. Plotinus's ideas would greatly influential kabbalah or the Jewish mystical tradition, as we will show when we turn to our third creation story.

It was under the influence of the church that Western thinking eventually rejected these mystical and hermetic ideas. The belief was that by accepting the presence of occult forces and spiritual realities in the universe, the power of God was compromised. To say that stars, planets, or even animals and rocks had certain occult abilities was to say that there were aspects of the universe that God did not control. To quote social critic Morris Berman, "By attributing power to matter itself, the Hermetic tradition had denied the power of God, Who should rightly be seen as Governor of the world, not immanent in it."[6]

To show that God was all powerful, the created universe had to become devoid of spirit, or as some have pointed out, disenchanted. Sociologist Max Weber called this the disenchantment of the world. As Weber wrote, "[Modernity is] the knowledge or the belief that, *if one only wanted to*, one *could* find out any time that there are in principle no *mysterious, incalculable powers at work*, but rather that one could in principle master everything through calculation. But that means the disenchantment of the world."[7] From this vision of a disenchanted physical world, modern science was born.

It was a third view that won out in this three-way contest described by Easlea. God was all powerful and therefore matter was totally passive. The universe was simply matter in motion. There were no mystical nor occult forces at work in the world, but matter moved by laws of motion which could be described by mathematics. The ultimate goal of science was to give a complete description of this matter in motion. This will become the basis of materialism which we will study in the second part of this book. But let's return to our dualist vision, which says that there is a second substance besides matter.

---

6. Berman, *Reenchantment*, 110.

7. Weber, *"Science as a Vocation,"* 13.

Dualists accept the reality of souls, spiritual entities not made of matter. The roots of the belief in the soul goes back to chapter 2 of Genesis: "God formed man from the dust of the ground and breathed into him a breath of life" (Genesis 2:7). The Hebrew word for the human soul is *neshama*, a term that literally means "breath." (Later when we study Jewish mysticism, we will learn that there are multiple Hebrew terms for the multiple levels of the human soul.) In one of the wisdom books of the Bible, Ecclesiastes, we will learn that at death, "The dust returns to the earth from whence it came, but the spirit returns to God who gave it" (Ecclesiastes 12:7). This uses an alternative term *ruach*, literally "wind" for the soul. We see that there are two types of substance in the world that God created—body and soul or matter and spirit. This creates the biggest philosophical problem for dualism—how can two different substances interact with one another.

Matter and Spirit

According to the dualist interpretation of reality we have two kinds of reality, two substances, to use Aristotle's term. There is matter, the physical world that works in accordance with the laws of physics. According to Descartes, matter is *res extensa*—something that takes up space. Then we have a second substance, mind or spirit, which is *res cogitans*—manifested in thought. Mind does not take up space. Also, mind does not work by physical laws but rather by free will. They are two very different kinds of things. Nonetheless, they interact with one another. Matter influences mind and mind influences matter. The difficult question for all dualists is, how is the interaction of two different substances possible?

Let me share one example of the problem with this dualist vision. Matter works by physical laws, including the law of conservation of energy. No new energy can be added to a closed physical system. And yet, when I use my mind to decide to move my arm, something nonphysical (my mind) is affecting something physical (my arm). A nonmaterial entity is adding energy to the material world. One can perhaps answer that my thoughts work by the energy in my brain, and therefore no new energy is entering the system. But it is difficult to see precisely how this works.

Dualists must answer this question of mind-body interaction. Descartes tried. He claimed that the pineal gland, at the base of the brain, was the place where mind and body meet. Today we know that Descartes was wrong; there is nothing mental about the pineal gland. It is an endocrine gland that produces serotonin, which affects sleep patterns. If we reject Descartes's answer, how do body and mind interact?

Let me mention one answer often given by dualists. This is based on the work of the rationalist philosopher Gottfried Wilhelm Leibniz (1646–1716). Leibniz was not a dualist but more a kind of idealist, as we will show later in this book. In fact, process philosophy, which we will explore in a later chapter, is partially based on Leibniz's theory. Leibniz believed the universe was made of bits of consciousness, which he called monads. Each monad was unaware of every other monad. Yet all these monads work together so perfectly that it makes this "the best of all possible worlds." Voltaire had Leibniz in mind when he mocked philosophy in his novel *Candide*, where disaster after disaster occurs and Professor Pangloss declares that "all is for the best in this best of all possible worlds." Pangloss is modeled on Leibniz.

How can Leibniz's monads work together if they are all unaware of each other's existence? The answer Leibniz gives is what he called pre-established harmony. God creates the monads to work together. Each has been established from the very beginning to act in harmony with one another, thus creating Leibniz's "best of all possible worlds." And this points toward an answer to the dualist dilemma. Remember that we are dealing with an all-powerful God here. Body and mind or matter and spirit work together because God causes them to work together. My mind says move my arm. God knows what my mind is thinking, so God causes my arm to move. An all-powerful God can do anything. God can make my mind and my body, two very different substances, work in harmony.

Of course, many would believe that pinning everything on God creates a kind of cop-out. It is a "God of the gaps" argument; God is the answer to all the unanswered questions. God is a temporary fill in until we come up with a better answer. And yet, for theists God is the best answer. God is all powerful and can do anything, including create harmony between bodies and souls.

Theism and the Soul

Central to theism is the dualistic belief, mentioned at the beginning of this chapter, that we have a body and we have a soul. The soul existed before we were born, was placed in the body when we were born, and will continue to exist after we die. Mainstream Jews, Christians, and Muslims all accept these teachings. But there are multiple questions. If the souls existed before we were born, when were they created? When does God place them in our bodies? And when does God remove them from our bodies? Where do our souls go after we die? Do they come back into our body once again, as taught by the doctrine of resurrection? Or are they given a new body through reincarnation, a doctrine of Eastern religions but also of Jewish mystics?

This idea of a soul as an actual entity, fundamental to theistic religion, is never mentioned explicitly in the Bible. The Bible simply speaks of the *neshama*, or breath of God: "God formed man from the dust of the earth, and breathed into his nostrils a breath of life, and man became a living soul" (Genesis 2:7). Each of the words used by the Bible for soul—*nefesh, ruach, neshama*—come from a root meaning "wind" or "breath." The breath of God animates not only humans but other animals. When we die, the body goes back to the ground and the breath returns to God: "The dust returns to the ground from whence it came, and the spirit returns to God who gave it" (Ecclesiastes 12:7).

There is nothing in the Bible about the existence of a soul going to some eternal life after death. The Bible simply says that when we die, we are gathered to our ancestors. When we die, we go to sleep with our fathers. Where does this popular image of the soul come from? The answer is that it comes from the Greeks, and in particular, Plato. Plato in his dialog *Phaedo*, which tells of the death of Socrates, seeks to prove the existence of the soul. The soul comes from the perfect World of the Forms, and returns this World of the Forms after death. That is why Socrates did not fear his own death, but actually looked forward to drinking the hemlock. Plato brings a number of proofs for the soul. Perhaps the strongest is that we humans have certain innate knowledge, knowledge of things we never learned but that we recall from before we were born. In another dialogue, Plato speaks of a slave who, with no training in mathematics, was able to prove the Pythagorean theorem. The rationalist school of philosophy, which builds on Plato, claims that humans have certain innate knowledge. This knowledge came to us before we were born.

The Platonic idea of the soul was accepted by the church father Augustine of Hippo (354–430), who sought to combine Platonic and biblical thought. In a similar way, the early Jewish philosopher Philo spoke about the existence of a perfect soul dwelling in an imperfect body. To quote Philo, "For each of us has come into this world as into a foreign city, in which before our birth we had no part, and in this city he does sojourn, until he has exhausted his appointed span of life."[8] These ideas of a soul coming into this world, foreign to the Bible, made their way into Western religion. It is part of the Greek interpretation of reality.

Of course, the Greeks believe that the world had always existed. To Plato, the souls come from an eternal world of the forms. To Aristotle, there

8. Philo, "On the Cherubim," 40.

was not a moment of creation but rather, the world always existed. But for the Abrahamic religions, the world was created by God and therefore had a temporal beginning. Souls must also have been created by God. When? Let me quote a fascinating passage from the *Zohar*, the great book of Jewish mysticism:

> At the time when God desired to create the universe, it came up in His will before Him, and He formed all the souls which were destined to be allotted to the children of men. The souls were all before Him in the forms which they were afterwards destined to bear inside the human body. God looked at each one of them, and He saw that many of them would act corruptly in the world. When the time of each arrived, it was summoned before God, who said to it: "Go to such and such a part of the universe, enclose thyself in such and such a body." But the soul replied: "O sovereign of the universe, I am happy in my present world, and I desire not to leave it for some other place where I shall be enslaved and become soiled." Then the Holy One (blessed be He) replied: "From the day of thy creation thou hast had no other destiny than to go into the universe whither I send thee." The soul, seeing that it must obey, sorrowfully took the way to earth and came down to dwell in our midst.[9]

Rabbinic tradition has a similar teaching. God has a storehouse of souls which he keeps in a place called *guf* (ironically, the word means "body"). The Talmud teaches, "R. Asi taught that the Messiah will not arrive until all the souls are used up in *guf*."[10] According to this image, God created souls and one by one God puts them in bodies. In the daily prayers Jews say, "The soul that You gave me is pure. You created it, You formed it, You put it in me, You guard it in me, and in the future you will take it from me, and then return it to me at a future time." Note the hint of the idea of bodily resurrection, vital not only to Judaism but to Christianity and Islam. The Greeks would never countenance bodily resurrection, the hope that a person will come back from the perfect World of the Forms to this corrupt world.

What happens to souls after we die? Jewish tradition speaks of *gan eden* (the Garden of Eden or paradise) and of *gehinnom* (literally the valley of *Hinom*, a valley outside Jerusalem where the Moabites used to sacrifice children). But neither of these Jewish visions of heaven or hell is as strongly developed as in Christianity or Islam. *Gehinnom* is a place of punishment, but the maximum sentence is twelve months, and there is no punishment

---

9. *Zohar* II 96b.
10. *Babylonian Talmud Yebamot* 62a.

on Shabbat. *Gan eden* is kept a bit vague, although we have one teaching from the rabbinic sage Rav, "This world is not like the World to Come. In the World to Come there is no eating and no drinking, no sexual activity and no business, no jealousy, hatred, or rivalry. Rather the righteous sit with their crowns on their heads and delight in the divine presence."[11] In my humble opinion, it sounds lovely to exist in this world, for a day or two. But I cannot imagine it for eternity. Maimonides speaks of an eternity of philosophical contemplation, which some individuals might find appealing. But the important Jewish idea, emphasized by the rabbis, is that the World to Come is not forever. We are coming back to this world.

Rabbinic tradition speaks of resurrection of the body. In fact, according to rabbinic thought, whoever denies resurrection of the dead from the Torah will have no place in the World to Come.[12] This idea has made it into our daily liturgy, where we praise God as *mechiyei hametim* (who brings the dead to life). Mystics took this idea in a slightly different direction, believing in reincarnation (*gilgul*) rather than resurrection. But they all agree that we are coming back into this world, getting a body once again. And by getting a body, we will be able to fulfill mitzvot and continue our purpose in this world. These ideas point to the importance of transforming this world rather than the world to come.

These teachings point in a particular direction, away from the centrality of the unembodied soul. Souls need bodies to do their work in this world, just as bodies need souls. Of course, this entire image is going to raise serious questions for many philosophers. Gilbert Ryle called it the myth of "the ghost in the machine." As we shall see later, there are alternative understandings of the relationship between the body and soul other than this one described by classic dualism.

There is one more activity that we can attribute to God. It is God who puts the souls in the bodies to begin with. It was God who breathed a living soul into the man he created from the dust of the earth. But this raises another complex question. At what level of complexity does God put a soul in a body? Descartes believed that only humans have souls. The rest of the animal kingdom is soulless, mere robots or automatons. Nonetheless, most of us believe that animals have souls, some level of mind or consciousness. But if dogs and cats have souls, what about birds? Fish? Lizards? Insects? Bacteria? Viruses? How low do we go? Is there a minimum level of brain complexity needed for a soul to enter a living thing?

---

11. *Babylonian Talmud Berachot* 17a.

12. *Mishnah Sanhedrin* 10:1.

This entire question points to the old story of the speaker who taught, "The world stands on an elephant, which is on the back of a turtle." A woman raises her hand, "What is the turtle standing on?" The man answers, "On the back of another turtle." The woman raises her hand again, "What is that turtle standing on?" The speaker, becoming frustrated, said, "Lady, it is turtles all the way down."

This simple story points to the absurdity that can mark classical theism and philosophical dualism. God created both bodies and souls *ex nihilo*, from nothing. Jewish tradition teaches that God has a storehouse of souls that God places in bodies. The end of time will come when God runs out of souls. When brains reach some level of complexity, God places a soul within it. By pre-established harmony, God causes the soul and the body to work together. And when the body dies, the soul returns to God.

In parts two and three of this book we will look at alternate creation stories, including alternate ways to look at the soul. But for the next three chapters we need to explore three important ideas in this theistic vision. First, does God cause the laws of nature to change by creating miracles? Second, if God created the universe, why did he do such a poor job? How do we account for evil in the world? And third, is God the source of ethics?; are certain actions right and wrong because God says they are right and wrong? For the next three chapters we will look at three issues raised by classical theism: miracles, evil, and ethics. These chapters will suggest that the theistic vision of creation, accepted by Jews, Christians, and Muslims, is not as simple as we would like.

CHAPTER 2

Miracles—Does God Change Nature?

The Talmud tells the story of a man whose wife died, leaving a new baby to feed. The man was too poor to afford a wet nurse. He prayed to God and a miracle occurred. He developed breasts like a woman and was able to nurse his infant. Rabbi Joseph said, "Come and see what a great man this was that a miracle was done on his behalf." Abaye disagreed, "On the contrary, come and see what an unworthy man this was that he made God change the laws of creation."[1]

In preparing to write my dissertation, I had many long talks with the philosophy professor, who was head of my committee. She is an expert on phenomenology, a branch of philosophy that deals with how the mind perceives the universe. We spoke of how classical theism, the view that God intervenes in the universe, had given way to deism, the view that God created the universe but has ignored it ever since. Often this gives way to atheism, the view that there is no God at all.

My professor had strong views opposed to deism. She called this theory, popular among Enlightenment thinkers, "God as deadbeat dad."

---

1. *Babylonian Talmud Shabbat 53b.*

Do Miracles Happen?

In the previous chapter we spoke about the kind of world an omnipotent God had created. We explored three different approaches. The medieval followers of Aristotle believed that it was a world where everything had its place and moved according to its final purpose. The hermetic and mystical thinkers of the Renaissance believed that it was a world filled with spiritual entities that moved according to a variety of sympathies and antipathies. In the end, these views were seen by religious authorities as a compromise on God's ultimate power. The modern view grew of a passive creation set in motion by God, a universe that worked according to laws God had established at the beginning of creation. God created the world and only God has the power to make changes in the laws that God had ordained.

This brings us to the fascinating question of miracles. If the world runs according to natural laws ordained by God, does God now and again change or overturn those laws? Does God cause a walking staff to turn into a snake, and then eat other staffs that have also turned into snakes? Does God cause a sea to part with walls on either side and dry land in the middle, as the book of Exodus describes? Does God cause a donkey to talk back to its master as in the story of Balaam in the book of Numbers? Does God cause the walls of a city to come tumbling down from the blast of trumpets as described in the book of Joshua? Does God cause the sun to stand still in the sky, or King Saul to communicate with the dead Samuel, or Elijah to go up to heaven in a fiery chariot? Can God make holy oil sufficient for only one day burn for eight days, the basis of the Hanukkah story? And if these events really happened, does God cause a person to be miraculously healed from a terminal disease in response to our prayers? Does God work miracles?

Classical theists would say yes, miracles do happen. If God is all-powerful and God created the laws of nature, then God has the ability to overturn those laws of nature. The Hebrew word for nature is *teva*, which comes from a Hebrew root which originally meant to sink or to drown. Perhaps nature means that God is sunk below, hidden below the surface. Most of the time God remains hidden, allowing the world to function according to the laws of nature. But God designed these laws of nature. And now and again God comes out of hiding to set aside the laws of nature, to perform a miracle.

Classical theism teaches that God set in motion the laws of nature. The world passively runs according to these laws. But God, being all powerful, now and again chooses to change these laws. God chooses to reach out from this hidden place and bring about a miracle. We humans can only react with wonder at God's greatness. Jews bless God on Hanukkah and Purim with the words, "Who did miracles for our ancestors in those days and in our own day." Jewish law says that if you visit a place where a miracle took place, you should say a blessing thanking God "for doing a miracle for me in this place." On Hanukkah we play with a dreidel, a little spinning top, whose letters spell out the phrase "a great miracle happened there." Theistic religions such as Judaism, Christianity, and Islam are built around God intervening in nature.

Nonetheless, modern thinking is skeptical about the presence of such miracles. The philosopher David Hume (1711–1776) wrote about miracles in his classic work *Enquiry Concerning Human Understanding*. Hume was an empiricist who believed that all knowledge comes through experience. Regarding a miracle, Hume said that there are two possibilities. Either we can believe that nature took its usual course and obeyed its own laws, which we know to be true through our experience. Or else we can believe that the laws of nature were suspended, something that we can only know through eyewitness testimony. Given the choice between believing such testimony and believing our own experience of how nature works, the logical choice is to believe that God did not change the laws of nature. There are no miracles. To quote Hume, "A miracle is a violation of the laws of nature; and as a firm and unalterable experience has established these laws, the proof against a miracle, from the very nature of the fact, is as entire as any argument from experience can possibly be imagined."[2]

It is true that Hume was a skeptic, not just about miracles but about almost everything. He denied anything that cannot be directly experienced, including causation. He believed that ethics were mere sentiments, not provable through observing nature. As he famously said, "You cannot learn an ought from an is." Hume even denied the existence of God; at the end of his life, others tried unsuccessfully to convince him to repent. Hume basically taught that we can only know as true what we can see with our own eyes, including the laws of nature. And most of us do not see miracles with our own eyes.

Another philosopher who taught some wisdom about miracles was Benedict Spinoza (1632–1677), born Jewish but rejected by the Jewish community. Spinoza, like Descartes and Leibniz, came from a rationalist tradition. Unlike the empiricists, rationalists taught that knowledge comes through the mind rather than through experience. Spinoza gave the world some brilliant ideas, and for his efforts was excommunicated at the age of

2. Hume, *Enquiry*, 58.

twenty-three from the Amsterdam Jewish community. (One of my goals as a rabbi is to welcome Spinoza back into the community.)

Regarding miracles, Spinoza taught that people look for God in the violations of natural law. God's existence is proved when seas part, the sun stands still, or a man is raised from the dead. When the world behaves according to its natural laws, there is no proof of God. To quote Spinoza, "They suppose, forsooth, that God is inactive as long as nature works in her accustomed order, and vice versa, that the power of nature and natural causes are idle as long as God is acting; thus, they imagine two powers distinct one from the other, the power of God and the power of nature."[3]

Spinoza said that these ideas are mistaken. God is seen not when the laws of nature are violated, but when nature runs according to its laws. God is seen in the laws of nature. In fact, Spinoza goes even further. He famously said *deus sive natura*—God is nature. Spinoza was a pantheist who believed that God and nature are the same, that we find God by studying nature. Of course, part of the reason that Spinoza was rejected by the Jewish community is that his pantheism (God is nature) does not fit into classical Judaism's theism (God is beyond and controls nature).

Nonetheless, I believe Spinoza makes an important point. We see God not in changes in the laws of nature, but within the laws of nature themselves. In fact, I believe that this is the more authentic Jewish definition of miracles. A miracle is not a change in nature but is actually part of nature. To see this, let us study the Jewish view of miracles.

A Different View of Miracles

At the beginning of the chapter we quoted the story from the Talmud about the man who grew breasts, so he could nurse his infant son. There was a disagreement between two rabbis—Rav Joseph and Abaye. Rav Joseph said how wonderful this man must be that a miracle happened on his behalf. Abaye answered, how unworthy a man he must be that God would change the laws of nature on his behalf. Abaye was one of the major sages of the Babylonian Talmud, and underlying his opinion is that changing the laws of nature is not desirable.

A similar idea comes out of another rather humorous story in the Talmud. There is a long tradition in Judaism of getting drunk on Purim. In fact, one should be sufficiently inebriated so that they cannot tell the difference between "blessed be Mordecai" and "cursed be Haman." (Mordecai

3. Spinoza, *Theologico-Political Treatise*, 81.

is the hero and Haman is the villain of the Purim story.) Two rabbis of the Talmud took this quite literally.

In the Talmudic story, Rabbah and R. Zeira were having a Purim feast together and they became quite drunk. Rabbah rose up and killed R. Zeira. The next day he prayed for mercy and was able to bring R. Zeira back to life. A year later Rabbah invited R. Zeira over for another Purim feast. R. Zeira declined, saying that we cannot assume that a miracle will happen once again.[4] In fact, Jewish tradition teaches "do not depend on miracles."[5] We do not build our lives around the idea that God is going to change the laws of nature for us.

This idea comes out explicitly in another Talmudic passage. The Talmud asks, if someone steals wheat and plants it, should that wheat not grow as punishment for the thief? The answer is that *olam keminhago noheg*—"the world behaves according to its laws." Similarly, if a man commits adultery with his neighbor's wife, should she not get pregnant and bless him with a child? The answer is that "the world behaves according to its laws."[6] There are laws of nature and God does not reach down and change those laws, even if there are very good ethical reasons to do so. God does not change nature for our benefit. The world continues to function according to its laws.

If the world functions according to natural laws, where do miracles fit in? Perhaps we ought to redefine miracle as a natural event, which can be scientifically understood, but that points to the presence of God. The Hebrew word for miracle is *nes*, a word that means "sign" or "banner." A miracle is a sign or banner that seems to point toward God, even though we can explain the event in a natural way. This seems closer to Spinoza's view that miracles are within nature.

There are various sources that seem to indicate that this is the Jewish view. Rabbis often quote a passage from the *Ethics of the Fathers* that speaks of the ten items created by God at twilight on the sixth day, immediately before the first Sabbath. These included such miraculous items as the place where the earth opened up to swallow Korach and his fellow rebels, the well that traveled with Miriam to give water to the people, the mouth of the donkey who spoke back to Balaam, the rod that turned into a snake, and the *shamir*, a worm that was able to write the Ten Commandments on two tablets.[7] What the rabbis are trying to say is that each of these seemingly miraculous items is built into nature itself.

4. *Babylonian Talmud Megillah* 7b.
5. *Babylonian Talmud Peachim* 64b.
6. *Babylonian Talmud Avoda Zara* 54b.
7. *Mishnah Avot* 5:7.

My favorite item in this list in *Avot* is a final addition, "some add the tongs made with tongs." What does this mean? In order to make metal tongs, one must hold them over a flame and shape them. They are held with another pair of tongs. But these tongs were also made by being held over the flames by an earlier pair of tongs. Where did the first set of tongs come from, the ones that started the process? This is the miracle built into nature. This idea can be applied to life itself. Proteins, the building blocks of life, require DNA to give them their structure. DNA requires proteins to build them. What came first, the proteins or the DNA? Something had to get it started, like the first set of tongs. This is natural and yet a miracle, something that points toward God. We will return to this passage in the chapter on evolution.

Let me share one more example from Jewish tradition. The miracle par excellence in the Torah is the parting of the sea. The Torah teaches that God caused a *ruach kadim aza*—"a strong East wind" to part the sea (Exodus 14:21). The Hebrew word *kadim* means "east," but it has a second meaning—"ancient." It was not an East wind but an ancient wind, a wind built into creation from the very beginning. The great Hasidic rebbe Levi Yitzhak of Berdichev taught, "God does not change or suspend the laws of nature in order to work miracles. The wind that divided the sea had been created for that purpose at the time of the creation of the world."

The miracles of the Bible are all totally natural events. Martin Buber told the story of two Israelites talking after the parting of the sea. One said, "I can explain it all. There was a low tide and a strong wind, nature was just right for us to pass through. When the Egyptians chased us with their chariots, the tides rose and their wheels became struck in the mud. That is why they drowned. There is a scientific explanation for all of it." His friend answered, "Never mind all that. This is my God and I will glorify Him."

Perhaps the person who best presented this Jewish view of miracles was Einstein. "There are two ways to live your life. One is as though nothing is a miracle. The other is as though everything is."

A Problem and a Solution

Now we have a definition of a miracle that can work for us. A miracle is not God reaching down and changing the laws of nature. Rather, a miracle is part of nature. It is when the laws of nature serve as a sign or banner, pointing to something beyond nature. The miracle is a natural event that points toward the presence of God.

If this is true, then we might say that all of nature points toward God, that all of nature is a miracle. Scientists speak about the anthropic principle, the principle that the natural world is fine-tuned so that life and consciousness will emerge. The constants of the universe are not there by random chance. If the numbers were slightly different, the universe as we know would not have evolved. If the gravitational force were the tiniest bit stronger, the stars would have collapsed long before they could have created the elements like carbon necessary for life. If the gravitational force were the tiniest bit weaker, the fusion at the heart of the stars would never have begun and the whole universe would be hydrogen gas. Like the Goldilocks story, the gravitational force is just right. So it is with the other constants of the universe, from the strength of the strong force that holds atoms together to the strength of the weak force that causes radioactive decay.

The universe seems to be designed in such a way that life would evolve, and this seems to imply a designer. Call that designer God. Of course, many scientists reject this anthropic principle. One popular claim accepted by many scientists today is that we live in a multiverse; there are billions and billions of universes, each with different constants. With so many universes, one must have the correct numbers. Even if the odds of winning the lottery are miniscule, sell enough tickets and somebody will win. If enough universes appear and disappear, one of them must be correct for life.

Judaism already hints at this idea. The midrash teaches that God made and destroyed many universes before making this one. God said, "The others do not please me, this one pleases me."[8] Certainly other universes with other laws are possible, but if they existed, we would not be here to write about them. This is sometimes called the weak anthropic principle. Nonetheless, to posit multiple universes so that we do not need to deal with a Creator strikes me as a violation of Ockham's razor. As mentioned in the introduction, the medieval philosopher William of Ockham (1287–1347) taught that one should not multiply entities beyond what is necessary, rather one should search for the simplest explanation for phenomena. It strikes me as far simpler to posit one universe fined-tuned from the beginning for us to evolve. This is called the strong anthropic principle.

Spinoza pointed us in this direction. I disagree with Spinoza's view that the universe, working by the laws of nature, is God. But I will say that the most authentic Jewish view is that the universe, working by the laws of nature, points toward God. God does not change the laws of nature to create miracles. Rather, the laws of nature themselves, uncovered by scientists over the generations, are the miracle.

8. *Genesis Rabbah* 3:7.

Nonetheless, this creates a problem for classical theists. If we say that God set the laws of nature in motion but does not intervene, is that not deism? Deism is the view that God created the world and then has ignored it. Many Enlightenment thinkers such as Thomas Jefferson were deists. Somehow this view is very unsatisfying. If someone is sick we like to believe that God will answer our prayers and intervene, perhaps even perform a miracle and cure the cancer. The belief that the world continues according to its nature without God's intervention leaves most people cold. We want to believe in miracles.

Let me propose a possible solution. In this section of the book, we are speaking about a dualist view of reality. The world is made of two substances, matter and spirit, body and soul. The matter or body works by natural scientific laws, which God does not change. But God can touch the soul or the spirit. A prayer for healing can be felt in the soul of someone who is ill. And that soul can perhaps play a role in the healing of the body. We know that diseases have both a physical and spiritual reality; we often use the term "psychosomatic" to refer to illness. *Psycho* comes from the Greek word for "mind" or "soul," while *somatic* comes from the Greek word for "body."

In a dualistic world as described by classical theism, God does not change the physical laws of nature. But God can touch the spirit. God can give our mind strength to move forward, or help us make the right choices. Twelve-step programs have long understood that we can turn to a Higher Power, God as we understand it, to overcome addiction. According to the Bible, when God created humanity He used the dust of the earth and then blew a breath of life. The dust of the earth is the physical; we have bodies that work by physical laws. But the breath of God is the spirit, the part of us that does not occupy space or follow the laws of physics. Perhaps we can believe in miracles as the place where God intervenes and touches our spirit. The Bible already hints at this when it speaks about people who were "moved by the spirit of God."

In part two of this book, we speak about materialism, where the world is a mere machine run by mechanical laws. There is no room for miracles in a spiritual view of reality. But in this section of theism, which sees a spiritual part of reality, we realize that the world is not merely a machine. There is a spiritual dimension to reality. Let me end this chapter with a piece of a Rosh Hashanah sermon I delivered a few years ago. I asked the question, do we live in a one-story universe or a two-story universe?

Professor Charles B. Jones of the Catholic University of America
in Washington, D.C., teaches an introduction to religion course

available in the Great Courses that I have found very helpful.[9] He said that non-religious people, atheists and secularists, materialists and humanists, live in a one-story universe. Religious people live in a two-story universe. Let me explain. What is a one-story universe? All that exists is matter and energy in space and time. All of reality is bits of material moving in space. There is nothing more.

But those who believe in a two-story universe say that there is something more. There is another dimension to reality beyond matter in motion. There is a spiritual reality, something that goes beyond the material. That spiritual reality has as many names as there are religions. To Jews it is God or *Yud-Hay-Vav-Hay*. To Jewish mystics it is *Ein Sof* and the *sefirot*. To Christians it is the logos. To Mormons it is Our Heavenly Father. To Muslims it is Allah. To Hindus it is Brahman. To Buddhists it is the Eightfold Way. To Daoists it is the Dao, simply the way. To Native Americans and other early religions, it is animism. To many people, Jews and non-Jews, it is angels and demons, spirits and a plethora of divine beings. To Jews, the second story of a two-story universe is also the *neshama* or soul, and the *olam haba* or world to come.

In such a universe, what is a miracle? The first story, the material world governed by the laws of physics, points to a second story. In this second story, the spiritual world, God intervenes. This is the world Jews have in mind when they pray three times a day toward the end of the *Amidah*, "for the miracles that He does for us every day, and for the wonders and kindnesses at all times, evening morning and afternoon."

We have a way to understand miracles. But this raises a more difficult question: Why does God allow evil to happen so that we have a need for such miracles? In the next chapter we will look at the problem of evil in a world created by a perfect God.

9. Jones, *Introduction*.

CHAPTER 3

Evil—Could God Have Made
a Better World?

The university professor challenged his students with this question. Did God create everything that exists? A student bravely replied, "Yes, he did!" The professor responded, "If God created everything, then God created evil since evil exists, and therefore God is evil." The student became quiet before such an answer. The professor was quite pleased with himself and boasted to the students that he had proven once more that the religious faith was a myth.

Another student raised his hand and said, "Can I ask you a question, professor? Does cold exist?" "What kind of question is this? Of course it exists. Have you never been cold?" The students snickered at the young man's question. The young man replied, "In fact sir, cold does not exist. According to the laws of physics, what we consider cold is in reality the absence of heat."

The student continued, "Professor, does darkness exist?" The professor responded, "Of course it does." The student replied, "Once again you are wrong, sir; darkness does not exist either. Darkness is in reality the absence of light."

Finally, the young man asked the professor, "Sir, does evil exist?" Now uncertain, the professor responded, "Of course as I have already said. We see it every day" To this the student replied, "Evil does not exist sir, or at least it does not exist unto itself. Evil is simply the absence of good. It is just like darkness and cold, a word that man has created to describe the absence of good. God did not create evil. It's like the cold that comes when there is no heat or the darkness that comes when there is no light."

The professor sat down. The young man's name: Albert Einstein.

I have reached an age in my life when many of my contemporaries are going in for joint replacements. They need new hips, new shoulders, and most common, new knees. I am one of the lucky ones; my joints are still working. But then I was never very athletic: I never played intensive basketball when I was young. Athletics has a delirious effect on joints. But as I see my friends recovering from surgery, one question keeps coming to mind: Couldn't God have made a better knee?

I remember visiting one of my members at a major hospital near downtown Ft. Lauderdale after his knee replacement surgery. I became totally lost trying to find the patient's room. The hospital was a large, sprawling complex, with multiple buildings joined together by various corridors. There were numerous elevators and stairways, all appearing disjointed. The hospital, one of the best in my area, was not carefully designed. It grew organically, new buildings being attached to old buildings. When it was time to build a new section of the hospital, they did not tear down the old section. They simply built where they could and attached it where they must. And so the hospital grew, organically, in a disjointed way. This seemed a perfect metaphor for how life grew on earth, not by careful design but slowly and organically.

Theodicy

It is not clear whether the apocryphal story attributed to Albert Einstein at the beginning of this chapter is true. Einstein was more a pantheist than a theist, more a believer in Spinoza than Moses. Still the story makes a good point about evil, and that is why it has been around for years. Several years ago I even used it in a high holiday sermon.

Some people would claim that our knee joints, and all the other parts of us, work as well as they possibly could. The world is as good as it could possibly be. In fact, the rationalistic philosopher Gottfried Leibniz, already mentioned in chapter 1, taught that "we live in the best of all possible worlds." The Enlightenment novelist Voltaire (1694–1778) made great fun of Leibniz in his classic novel *Candide*. Candide is a young man who faces tragedy after tragedy, as his teacher Professor Pangloss, modeled after Leibniz, keeps insisting that "everything is for the best in this best of all possible worlds." *Candide* is not only one of the most popular novels in history, but it became a Broadway musical composed by Leonard Bernstein.

It seems obvious that we do not live in the best of all possible worlds. In fact, we live in a world filled with pain and suffering, with all kinds of evil. Buddhists share the tale of the founder of their religion. Siddhartha

Gautama (born about 563 BCE), who would become the Buddha, born into an aristocratic family, was kept protected as a child by his father. He tried to prevent Siddhartha from seeing the reality of the outside world. But when Siddhartha grew a bit older and went outside into the world, he saw the pain of poverty, illness, and death. He became a wanderer, trying to find the proper path amidst the suffering of life. The man who would become the Buddha or enlightened one finally came up with the four noble truths that form the basis of the Buddhist religion. The first of these truths is, life is *dukkha*—suffering. Pain and loss are part of life in this world. God could have made a better knee. To the Buddha, the key to living in a world of suffering is to learn to let go of desire.

Buddhism is a non-theistic religion. But Western religions such as Judaism are theistic, picturing an all-powerful God who created the world. The biggest religious question facing classical theism is the question of suffering, why is there evil in the world? If God is all-knowing and all-powerful, why do we live in a world where bad things happen to good people? The problem of evil is the primary argument used by non-believers to prove that God, at least God as traditionally understood, could not exist. To quote the great skeptic David Hume, who we met in the previous chapter, "Is he (God) willing to prevent evil, but not able? Then he is impotent. Is he able but not willing? Then he is malevolent. Is he both able and willing? Whence then evil?"[1]

Of course, theists throughout history have come up with solutions. We will explore some of those suggested solutions. But it is vital that we tackle the problem of evil in the world, and how to reconcile it with an all-powerful and all-good God. The name for this problem is theodicy, the justification of God in the face of evil and suffering.

The problem of theodicy, how to justify God in the presence of evil and suffering, is as old as the Bible itself. The entire book of Job deals with this question. Job is an extremely good man who has been blessed with wealth and many children. God calls together his hosts of angels, including the adversarial angel know as *Ha-Satan*, and speaks about Job's faithfulness. (The word "Satan," which has come to mean the devil or a malevolent force in the world, is a later development, particularly in Christianity. In the Bible, Satan merely serves as the adversarial angel, somewhat like a prosecuting attorney before God.) *Ha-Satan* responds that of course Job is good and pious, look at how he has been rewarded in life. Let me bring punishment upon Job and we will see how long his goodness will last.

---

1. Hume, *Dialogues*, 44.

Ha-Satan brings a series of horrible calamities on Job. He loses all his wealth. He loses all his children. Finally, he is afflicted with a skin disease. Job's wife says to her husband, "Curse God and die" (Job 2:9). But even now Job refuses. "Should we accept the good from God and not the bad" (Job 2:10). Job also said the words I use at every funeral, "The Lord giveth and Lord taketh away, praised be the name of the Lord" (Job 1:21).

Three of Job's friends come to sit by him and comfort him. Eventually a fourth friend joins them. Job speaks first, crying out to God and calling God to a trial. He proclaims his innocence and the injustice of his suffering. Eventually he will say, "O that I knew where to find him, that I might come even to his seat. I would order my cause before him, and fill my mouth with arguments" (Job 23:3-4). His friends are hardly a comfort. They proclaim the ancient religious idea, still believed by many religious people, that there is no suffering without sin. The first of the friends, Eliphaz, declares, "Remember I beg you, whoever perished being blameless? Or where were the righteous cut off? As I have seen, those who plow iniquity and sow wickedness, reap the same" (Job 4:7-8). Job's friends insist that suffering has a purpose. It is punishment for sin.

Job disagrees with his friends and asks God to respond to his cries. And eventually God does respond. But God's response to Job brings us no closer to the answer of why there is suffering in the world. "The Lord answered Job from the whirlwind and said . . . Where were you when I laid the foundations of the earth?" (Job 38:1,4). God delivers a long speech that overwhelms Job, and in the end Job simply says, "Therefore I loathe myself, and repent in dust and ashes" (Job 42:2). The book ends as it began, with Job having everything—his wealth, his children, and his health—restored. But ultimately the book is unsatisfying; the question of theodicy has not been answered.

The rabbis of the Talmudic age realized the problem raised in the book of Job. In *Pirkei Avot*, known in English as *The Ethics of the Fathers*, we learn, "Rabbi Yannai said, 'It is not in our hands to understand the tranquility of the wicked nor the suffering of the righteous.'"[2] The prosperity of the wicked and the suffering of the righteous are the greatest challenge to classical theism. David Hume seems to speak the truth: If God is all-powerful and if God is all-good, why is there evil in the world?

I have read the work of rabbis who agree with Job's friends. All evil is a punishment for sin in this world. These rabbis build on the notion of the world to come, a place where the soul continues to survive. Everybody sins in this world. People who are punished in this world will get their full

---

2. *Mishnah Avot* 4:15.

reward in the world to come. On the other hand, people who do not suffer in this world will receive the full brunt of the punishment in the next. One way or the other, in this world or the next, full justice will be meted out. God will punish us, whether now or in a future world, measure for measure.

The Talmudic passage that demonstrates this idea most clearly is the story of the Rabbi Elisha ben Abulya, who forsook his Judaism and became a heretic.[3] How did he lose his faith? There was a boy whose father told him to climb a tree and take a baby bird, but first send away the mother bird. The Torah teaches that if one honors their father and mother they will have a long life. The Torah also teaches that if one sends away the mother bird before taking the baby bird, they will have a long life. But in this sad case, the boy fell out of the tree and died.[4] When Elisha ben Abulya saw this he immediately gave up his faith. He cried out, *leit din v'leit dayan*—"there is no judge and no justice." The rabbis responded that he was wrong, the reward and the punishment take place in the next world. Rabbi Milton Steinberg, in his wonderful novel *As a Driven Leaf*, portrays Elisha ben Abulya and powerfully tells this story of the rabbi who lost his faith.

It is a popular idea among most religious people that the righteous are rewarded and the sinners are punished. But both the reward and the punishment take place in the next world. The reward will take place in *Gan Eden*, literally "the Garden of Eden," the Jewish vision of heaven. The punishment will take place in *Gehinnom* "the valley of Hinom," a valley outside Jerusalem where the ancient Moabites used to sacrifice their children. This is the Jewish vision of hell. But unlike Dante's Inferno, the maximum punishment in this Jewish hell is twelve months. For many people this solves the problem of evil. If people suffer in this world, it means that their reward will be that much greater in the next world. Ultimately, justice will prevail.

The Talmud already challenges this idea that suffering is good because it leads to a greater reward in the next world. "Rabbi Hiyya bar Abba fell ill and Rabbi Johanan went in to visit him. He said to him: Are your sufferings welcome to you? [For they will give him a greater reward in the next world.] He replied: Neither they nor their reward. He said to him: Give me your hand. He gave him his hand and he raised him."[5] Pain and suffering can never be precious, even if it leads to a greater reward in the next world. It would be better if this world were without suffering. So once again the question remains, why evil?

3. At the beginning of chapter 11, on mysticism, we will learn of the role mystical speculation played in Elisha ben Abulya's apostasy.

4. *Babylonian Talmud Hullin* 142a.

5. *Babylonian Talmud Berachot* 5b.

To respond to David Hume, perhaps we live in a world where God is not all-powerful. Or perhaps we live in a world where God is not all-good. Or if God is all-powerful and all-good, perhaps what we consider evil is not really evil. Let us explore each of these possibilities.

Perhaps God Is Not All-Powerful

In 1981 Rabbi Harold Kushner published his best-selling book *When Bad Things Happen to Good People*. He wrote it after the tragic death of his fourteen-year-old son Aaron from Progeria, the rapid-aging disease. Kushner admitted that through much of his early rabbinic career he had spoken the standard line of Jewish tradition, that God must have his reasons. But Kushner realized that God's reasons could never account for the suffering and death of a child. Perhaps it was time to rethink this ancient theology. In doing so, Kushner brought comfort to countless people who read his book.

At the heart of the book is the idea that perhaps God is not all-powerful. Things happen in the world that God cannot prevent. God may strengthen us and help us cope with evil. God may even cry with us. But God cannot prevent evil. Let me quote Kushner: "I believe in God. But I do not believe the same things about Him that I did years ago, when I was growing up or when I was a theological student. I recognize His limitations. He is limited in what He can do by the laws of nature and by the evolution of human nature and human moral freedom. I no longer hold God responsible for illnesses, accidents, and natural disasters, because I realize that I gain little and lose so much when I blame God for these things. I can worship a God who hates suffering but cannot eliminate it, more easily than I can worship a God who chooses to make children suffer and die, for whatever exalted reason."[6]

Kushner is making a radical break with classical theism. But we have already seen a hint of his ideas in the previous chapter. There we learned that nature goes about its business, and God does not reach down and change those laws of nature. Sometimes nature can be cruel, when it brings a tsunami or causes birth defects. But nature works according to its own inexorable laws, and God does not intervene. In a similar way, humans have been given free will to practice good or evil. God may cry when the Holocaust or 9/11 happens, but again God does not intervene. God allows humans to act freely, even when they act cruelly.

The idea of a God who is not all-powerful has a place in Jewish tradition. Let us turn for a moment to kabbalah, or Jewish mysticism, particularly as conceived by the great sixteenth-century mystic Isaac Luria. We

---

6. Kushner, *When Bad Things*, 134.

will explore Luria's ideas further in the chapter on mysticism. Luria built an alternative creation story based on the idea of God who deliberately limited him/herself. (More than the classical conception of God at the beginning of Genesis, which is very masculine, the God of Luria is far more feminine. In Genesis God creates a universe outside himself, much as a father sires a child. In Lurianic kabbalah, God creates a universe within herself, much as a mother develops a child.)

Lurianic kabbalah begins with an image of God deliberately contracting, creating an empty space within God's very self. Kabbalists use the term *tzimtzum*, meaning "contraction." By contacting, God left sparks of light (*nitzitzot*) throughout the universe. Bits of God permeated everything, held in vessels called *kelim*. But the light was too powerful for the vessels, and the vessels shattered, scattering the light everywhere. The breaking of the vessels is called *shvirat hakelim*.

With the shattering of the vessels, the sparks were hidden everywhere, often within coverings called *kelipot*. It is these *kelipot* that are the source of evil in the world. They cover up the brokenness of God. Out of this comes one of the most powerful ideas not simply in Jewish mysticism but among Jewish thinkers of all persuasions. Human beings in general, and the Jewish people in particular, have the ability to uncover those holy sparks and return them to God. If God is broken, we have the ability to make God whole once again. The Hebrew word for this is *tikkun*, literally "repair." Our job is *tikkun olam*, to repair the world. Jews use the term *tikkun* all the time, unaware that it began in Safed as part of a rather arcane mystical tradition.

There is power in the idea that God is not all-powerful, that God is limited or perhaps even broken. Evil grows out of this brokenness. And we humans can fight evil by fixing the brokenness. In fact, our liturgy hints at this idea. Jews say the *Sh'ma* twice daily, a proclamation of faith saying, "Here O Israel, the Lord is our God, the Lord is One." But then Jews say in the *Alenu* prayer at the end of every service a verse from the prophet Zechariah, "On that day the Lord will be One and His Name will be One" (Zechariah 14:9). Is God One now, or will God be One someday in the future? God is broken now, but through our work, we can make God One sometime in the future.

Perhaps God Is Not All-Good

There is a verse in the book of Isaiah that the Lord is the God of everything. God "forms light and creates darkness, makes peace and creates evil" (Isaiah 45:7). The verse was written by a prophet who lived during the Babylonian exile, who scholars call Deutero-Isaiah (2nd Isaiah). One of the great concerns of this post-exilic prophet was to proclaim that there is one universal God, not the multiple gods of earlier sources. Deutero-Isaiah was the prophet who taught, "I am the Lord and there is no one else" (Isaiah 45:5). If there is only the one God who created everything, then God must have made both good and evil.

This verse from Isaiah quoted above has made it into the daily liturgy of Judaism, with one change of wording. Rather than say that "God creates evil," the daily prayerbook says that "God creates everything." Why did the rabbis who developed the liturgy change Isaiah's words? Perhaps they were uncomfortable having Jews articulate every day that God is the creator of evil. God is the creator of everything says the same thing, but in a less stark way. But Isaiah is trying to say that the one God creating everything that exists; since evil exists, God created evil. God is not all good.

What was Isaiah reacting to? Perhaps it was an inchoate idea, as prevalent in biblical times as today, that God is only responsible for the good. There is some other being, a second god or to use Plato's term, a demiurge, responsible for the evil. The idea can be seen in the 1986 Marlee Matlin movie about a hearing-impaired woman, *Children of a Lesser God*, for which Matlin won a best actress Oscar. The movie is based on a stage play by Mark Medoff of the same name. The idea is that since God is good, then some other being is responsible for evil. Someone hearing impaired or otherwise disabled must be the child of a lesser god.

This dualistic philosophy has a long history in human thought. (By dualism, we are not talking about the dichotomy between spirit and matter but of a dichotomy between a good creator and an evil creator. Scholars sometimes use the phrase *cosmological* dualism as opposed to *metaphysical* dualism. These two types of dualism come together in ancient Gnosticism which identifies spirit with the good and matter with the evil.)

Perhaps the oldest examples of such a dualistic religious system was Zoroastrianism, an early religion founded in Persia. The founder of Zoroastrianism, Zarathustra, lived about a hundred years before Deutero-Isaiah. Zarathustra speaks of the great cosmic battle between two gods, the god of good known as Ahura Mazda and the god of evil known as Angra Mainyu. (Yes, the automobile company Mazda was named after this good god.) Humans must make a choice of which god to follow. It is noteworthy that the philosopher Friedrich Nietzsche made his famous statement "God is Dead" in his book *Thus Spoke Zarathustra*.

There are not many Zoroastrians left in the world today, and the communities that are left are concentrated in India. But the ideas behind this ancient faith were very influential throughout the ancient world. For example, in chapter 1 we mentioned Gnosticism, which is a belief that there is a hidden knowledge that can help the soul find release from this physical or material world. Gnosticism sees the material world as tainted with evil as opposed to a spiritual world that is good. The soul is trapped in this spiritual world. Perhaps Gnosticism is best summarized by a quote from the Jewish philosopher Hans Jonas, an important scholar of Gnosticism: "Life has been thrown into the world, light into darkness, the soul into the body. It expresses the original violence done to me in making me be where I am and what I am, the passivity of my choice-less emergence into an existing world which I did not make and whose law is not mine."[7]

The gnostic idea that the material world is a place of evil can also be seen in the writings of Plato. In his dialog on the creation story *The Timaeus*, Plato sees a world formed by a demiurge, a kind of lesser god discussed above. In any beginning college philosophy class, students learn Plato's famous allegory of the cave from *The Republic*. Plato compares this world to shadows reflected on a wall. People are chained down so that they can only see the shadows. Then one person escapes to the place where light is shining on various figures forming the shadows. To Plato this is the perfect World of the Forms, the ideal, unchanging world. The material world is corrupt and constantly changing, a reflection or a shadow thrown forth by the perfect world. The human soul comes from this perfect place, enters the material world, but one day will return once again to this perfect place. Plato's influence on the Abrahamic religions such as Judaism, Christianity, and Islam is clear. Once again we see a kind of dualism, where the spiritual is good and the material is bad.

So far these dualist ideas still view the good as superior to the evil. Light outweighs darkness. Zoroastrianism is considered a monotheistic religion, with one God and a powerful demonic force both present in the world. Gnosticism and Platonic thinking sees spirit as superior to matter. But a new teacher arose in Iran in the third century of the common era who taught a true dualistic cosmology, with powerful forces of both light and darkness. The founder of this school was a religious prophet named Mani (216–274 CE) and his theology is called Manichaeism. Manichaeism was extremely popular in the early centuries of the first millennium. In fact, Augustine of Hippo, before converting to Christianity and becoming its greatest early interpreters, was a devoted Manichaean.

Mani, in order to understand the existence of evil, denied God's omnipotence. God represented by light was opposed by an eternal evil power represented by darkness. The evil of the world, including natural evil like

7. Jonas, *Gnostic Religion*, 334–35.

earthquakes and hurricanes, came from this evil power. But it is not just nature who has this dual nature. The human soul also contains both the force of goodness and the force of evil, struggling within our very being. These ideas are very similar to the Jewish view of the struggle between the *yetzer hatov* (good inclination) and the *yetzer hara* (evil inclination). It even has parallels in Sigmund Freud's modern vision of the human psyche as a struggle between the id and the superego.

This idea of a struggle between the forces of good and the forces of evil continue right up to our own time. One thinks of the *Star Wars* series of movies, with the confrontation between the "force" and the "dark side." But modern religion has also developed this dualistic view. In the story of Job, we talked about one of God's angels being *HaSatan*, literally "the adversary." This adversary became God's fallen angel, renamed Lucifer and eventually becoming Satan. Belief in the devil or Satan as a force of evil is central to the religious view of many Christians. For example, the snake who convinced Eve to eat of the fruit of the tree was really Satan in disguise. This act of disobedience by Adam and Eve, urged on by Satan, became the source of the fall of the world and the beginning of evil. (An intriguing thought: Many of these ideas about "the fall" came from Augustine. One wonders if his early life as a Manichean still influenced his Christian outlook.)

We have discussed a cosmological dualism over several pages, a subject with a complicated history. Scholars are still arguing how Zoroastrianism, Gnosticism, Neoplatonism, and Manichaeism influenced each other, and what kind of influence they had on Judaism, Christianity, and Islam. But on some basis level, Judaism rejects this idea that there are separate forces of good and of evil in the world. Judaism would not say that spirit is good and matter is evil. After all, when God created the material world, the Torah says that God saw it was "very good." The world is one. And if evil is part of the world, than God created evil. This is what Isaiah, and what the Hebrew prayerbook are trying to teach. God made everything.

So how could God be all-good? The answer given by many theists is that what we humans call evil God calls good. We are seeing the world from our limited perspective. From God's point of view there is no evil.

Perhaps There Is No Evil

John Hick (1922–2012) is one of the most prominent Christian theologians in recent times. He built a theodicy (defending God in the face of evil) that rejected Augustine's vision that evil was caused by the fall of man. He based his theology more on the Eastern Father Irenaeus, who spoke of the ongoing continuous creation of humanity. According to Hick, evil has a role to play in what he calls "soul-making." The human soul is put into a world of sadness and suffering to slowly build itself toward a more idyllic future. Evil then serves a purpose, to help perfect humanity.

Hick's theology reminds me very much of a conversation I had early in my rabbinate. A woman from my congregation told me that I seemed very nice, but she was not yet ready to accept me as her rabbi. She said that I had not yet suffered enough. To be a full human being, a person has to be tested, to endure suffering in life. Jewish midrash shares a similar idea. When the Torah teaches that God tested Abraham, the midrash teaches, "R. Jonathan said, a potter does not examine defective vessels, because he cannot give them a single blow without breaking them. What then does he examine? Only the sound vessels, for he will not break them even with many blows. Similarly, the Holy One, blessed be He, tests not the wicked but the righteous."[8] Evil serves a divine purpose by making human beings the kind of people God wants them to be.

There is much appealing about Hick's theodicy. Nonetheless, it is difficult to say to someone who has endured a tragic loss that God is testing them to make them better people. I do not believe that when Rabbi Kushner and his wife lost their son, it was simply "soul building." Too often I hear people quote Nietzsche after a funeral, "What doesn't kill us makes us stronger." It has become a cliché. But somehow it seems of scant comfort. Still, the idea that evil is not really evil because it serves some divine purpose has a strong appeal to many who accept classic theism. Let us develop this idea further by looking more closely at evil.

Philosophers speak of two different kinds of evil—human evil and natural evil. Human evil is caused by human beings. Often people ask me, "How could a good God cause the Holocaust?" My answer is simply, "God did not cause the Holocaust. Human beings did." I suppose God could reach down from heaven and intervene. Perhaps God could have stopped those planes from flying into the World Trade Center on 9/11. But that is a peculiar view of God, one that has no respect for human free will.

One of the most important teachings of the Torah is that God gave humans free will. We can choose to do good or do evil. As far back as the Cain and Abel story, God says to Cain, "Sin crouches at the door; its urge is towards you, yet you can be its master" (Genesis 4:7). Unfortunately, Cain could not master his evil urge when he rose up and slew his brother Abel. Later Jewish tradition would teach that humans are born with a *yetzer hatov*

8. *Genesis Rabbah* 55:2.

(good inclination) and a *yetzer hara* (evil inclination). The goal in life is to control that evil inclination. "Ben Zoma said, Who is strong? Whoever controls their inclination?"[9]

Early on God realizes that humans can do great evil. "The Lord saw how great was man's wickedness on the earth, and how every plan devised by his mind was nothing but evil all the time" (Genesis 6:5). Yet God has given humans the freedom to choose. Even Pharaoh, where God hardened his heart, at first freely chose to prevent the Israelites from going free. Only after Pharaoh hardened his own heart did God finally harden his heart. If we do the wrong thing enough times, it becomes a habit, almost second nature, as if God made us that way.

Human evil is a natural result of human free will. Later in this book, when we study materialism, we will look at various philosophical approaches that deny human free will. But for the moment, we must accept that God gave us the right to choose. Sadly, too many of us choose to do evil. God can cry, but God does not intervene.

The more difficult issue is natural evil. How do we explain hurricanes, earthquakes, tornadoes, and tsunamis? How do explain birth defects, cancer cells, disease, and epidemics? Why did God create a world where terrible things happen, a world that does not differentiate between the innocent and the guilty? Could a benevolent God have created a less violent, more perfect universe?

I have found much wisdom in a book written by the Brazilian physicist and author Marcelo Gleiser titled, *A Tear at the Edge of Creation*. Gleiser writes, "I began to recognize that it is not symmetry but the presence of *asymmetry* that best represents some of the most basic aspects of nature. Symmetry may have its appeal but it is inherently stale; some kind of imbalance is behind every transformation."[10] Gleiser believes that we are mistaken when we look for wholeness and perfection in the universe. Rather, the universe is broken, and that very brokenness allows it to move forward. Gleiser sees a universe in process. But process must begin with pain.

At the beginning of time there were only hydrogen atoms. But those atoms must be destroyed through fusion, giving off energy and creating stars. And those stars must explode to create the larger chemicals, including carbon necessary for life. Matter must coalesce into planets, which must constantly be in motion for the process to move forward. Volcanoes, hurricanes, and tidal waves are all necessary to bring chemicals to the surface that will form life. Evolution is how life expands on the universe, but evolution

9. *Mishnah Avot* 4:1.

10. Gleiser, *Tear*, xiv.

requires mutations of genes and birth defects. Species die off so that other species can flourish, and species evolve through vicious competition. The same genetic mutations that allow evolution to move forward are the causes of birth defects and cancer.

We live in a material world that is constantly in motion, constantly progressing. But it is the brokenness that allows this process to take place. As mentioned earlier, scientists speak of broken symmetry. This sounds a lot like the broken vessels of Lurianic kabbalah, a brokenness that is the basis of progress. Luria's answer is not to cry out at God for the brokenness of the world. Rather, it is to become partners of creation, to try to fix the brokenness.

Perhaps Isaiah is right, that God is the creator of evil. God created human evil by giving humans free will and refusing to intervene when we misuse our power. God created natural evil by building a world based on brokenness, to use Gleiser's term, by putting tears in the edge of creation. But this leads to a mandate for human beings, to recognize the brokenness in the world, in God's very self, and begin the process of repairing the world.

CHAPTER 4

Ethics—Why Be Good?

When Socrates went to court, he met Euthyphro who was bringing a case against his father. Euthyphro told Socrates that he was bringing a capital case against his father for impiety, for defying the gods. His father had beaten a slave to death. Euthyphro said that this was the pious thing to do. Socrates asked Euthyphro what he meant by piety. Euthyphro answered that piety is obeying the will of the gods. Socrates responded that in a world of multiple gods, what if the gods disagree with one another? Euthyphro then changed his definition, saying piety is defying the will of all the gods. Socrates asked, so something is pious if it is what all the gods want? Yes, answered Euthyphro. Then Socrates asked his fundamental question of religion: Is something pious because the gods will it? Or do the gods will it because it is pious?

I teach a class in ethics at my local community college. On the first day of class, I always ask my students if the intentional murder of an innocent person is wrong. Of course, they all say yes. Then I ask them, why is it wrong? What makes the murder of innocents wrong? The answer is far more difficult than one might think.

One of the students will usually tell me that it is wrong because you might get caught. You might end up in jail, or even being executed, for murder. So it is wrong because of the consequences. I then ask, what if you knew for an absolute fact that you would not be caught, that you could get away with it? In that situation, is murder wrong?

I then ask my students a question: "Suppose you witnessed a bank robbery and saw one of the robbers drop a large bundle of money as he ran out of the bank. Suppose you knew that there were no witnesses and no security cameras around. Would you keep the money?" More than half my class usually says yes. I respond, "You are telling me that certain acts are wrong only if you might get caught?"

God and Ethics

Plato, in his great work *The Republic*, already raised the question whether ethics was simply about not getting caught. He put the question in the mouth of his brother Glaucon, arguing with Socrates. Glaucon tells the story, probably popular in Plato's time, of Gyges and the magical ring. He found the ring in a tomb uncovered by an earthquake and immediately pocketed it. Then Gyges discovered that the ring had magical powers; it had the power to make him invisible. While invisible, Gyges entered the palace, murdered the king, seduced the queen, and took over the kingdom. Being invisible allowed him to get away with it. Glaucon famously says, in this situation "no man can be imagined to be of such an iron nature that he would stand fast in justice." Glaucon teaches that it is human nature to get away with whatever we can get away with.

This ring with such magical powers has been prevalent in Western cultural history, from Richard Wagner's opera cycle *The Ring of the Nibelungen* to Tolkien's popular trilogy *The Lord of the Rings*. Socrates, in response to Glaucon, defends the human ability to remain ethical even if they know that they can get away with murder. Socrates famously says, "Knowledge leads to virtue." If we know the right thing to do, we will do the right thing. But was Socrates correct? How many of us know the right thing and do the wrong thing anyway? We even have a word for it: rationalization.

Returning to my class and the question why the murder of an innocent is wrong, someone usually says next, "murder is wrong because the Ten Commandments forbids it." One of the most popular ideas in our culture is that theistic religion is the source of morality. The novelist Fyodor Dostoyevsky says it literally in his great novel *The Brothers Karamazov*, "Without God, everything is permitted." In the section known as the Grand Inquisitor, the brother Ivan claims that without God everything is permitted, where the issue comes up among the brothers whether it is permissible to murder their evil father.

Is Dostoyevsky, a religious Christian, correct? Is religion the basis of ethics? Is right or wrong simply whatever God declares to be right or wrong? What about atheists—why should they be ethical? This is a fundamental question of the theistic view of religion. It is worthy of exploration.

The popular view that right and wrong are simply whatever God declares to be right and wrong is known by philosophers as divine command theory. It was the theory proclaimed in Plato's dialog *Euthyphro*, summarized at the beginning of this chapter. Euthyphro tells Socrates that piety is doing whatever the gods say. We can translate into a more biblical idiom—goodness is obeying God's command. Right and wrong is simply whatever God says is right and wrong. This was the view of Dostoyevsky mentioned above, that without God there is no right or wrong. Everything is permitted.

This was also the thinking of the early existentialist philosopher Soren Kierkegaard (1813–1855). Kierkegaard was an existentialist in his belief that we have the freedom to create ourselves. He taught that we are offered three choices in life. We can live the aesthetic life, simply seeking enjoyment and pleasure. We can live the ethical life, doing whatever is expected of us, going to church but not feeling any real passion. Kierkegaard loved to attack the nominal Christians in his native Copenhagen, those who went through the motions of religion but did not live in a relationship with God.

The third choice is what Kierkegaard called "the leap of faith." (Kierkegaard invented that phrase.) This is to set aside all scruples including ethical scruples and live in a total relationship with God. To Kierkegaard the ideal man of faith was the biblical Abraham, who was prepared to sacrifice his son Isaac because God commanded him. In his seminal book *Fear and Trembling*, Kierkegaard calls Abraham a "knight of faith," prepared to live before God with infinite resignation. One acts even if it is absurd. The ethical is whatever God commands, including sacrificing one's son. The life of faith is to live totally in the presence of God. Right and wrong are simply what God commands and nothing more.

Kierkegaard's interpretation of the binding of Isaac raises a deep religious question. Is being ethical doing whatever God commands? Many rabbis interpret the story of the binding of Isaac (*Akedah*) in a totally different way. For example, in my book *The Ten Journeys of Life*, I argue that Abraham failed the test. He should have argued with God, just as he argued with God to save the cities of Sodom and Gomorrah. Murder is wrong, even if we believe God commanded it. Even God is held to a standard of right and wrong. Abraham himself says to God, "Should the judge of all the earth not do justly" (Genesis 18:25).

In our own time, when people murder innocents, detonate bombs, and fly airplanes into buildings in the name of God, it seems crucial to reject divine command theory. Good and evil are not what God commands.

Some acts are evil, even if we believe God commanded these acts. Sadly, every religion including my own has a history of people acting cruelly in the name of God. At the time of the Roman destruction of the second Temple in Jerusalem, infighting killed many Jews in the besieged city. Jews would assassinate other Jews who disagreed with their interpretation of how to react to the Romans. Later the rabbis of the Talmud would teach that the Temple was destroyed because of *sinat hinam*, unjustified hatred. We cannot say that good and evil are simply whatever God calls good and evil when so much evil has been done in the name of God.

When my students say that murder is wrong because God says so, I raise another question. Before God said so, was murder wrong? What about the Cain and Abel story? When Cain killed his brother Abel, the Ten Commandments had not yet been given. The Noahide laws, given to Noah and including the prohibition of bloodshed, had not yet been given. In fact, in the Bible when Cain killed his brother Abel, nobody had ever died. Yet Cain is punished. He must have known that he had done something wrong even without an explicit commandment. Right and wrong must have existed before God said anything.

This is precisely Socrates's brilliant point to Euthyphro. To paraphrase Socrates, is an act right or wrong because God says so? Or does God say so because the act is right or wrong? Does ethics have some independent reality beyond what God says? In fact, can we hold God to this ethical standard that pre-existed him? I believe Socrates is correct. And I believe Abraham is correct when he tells God, the Lord of all the earth must act justly. Justice exists independent of God. And murder was wrong before God said anything. Murder is wrong even if people do not believe in God, and it is wrong even if people interpret God's will as condoning it.

The murder of innocent people is wrong. It would be wrong even if God does not exist. The fascinating question is why is it wrong? We will explore this issue through the rest of this chapter.

Culture and Ethics

I raise another question on the first day of my Introduction to Ethics class. In India they used to practice *Sati*, a tradition that when a man died, his widow would throw herself on the funeral pyre. When Britain colonized India they outlawed the practice. I believe it is still part of Indian tradition that is practiced in some rural areas to this day. I ask my students the question, was Britain correct in outlawing an Indian cultural practice?

Most of my students say that Britain was wrong, that they had no right to outlaw a practice that is part of another nation's culture. I then raised other cultural practices. The ancient Aztecs used to practice human sacrifice. Would it be right to outlaw that? Certain aboriginal people in northern Alaska used to allow their elders to walk off onto the ice rather than become a burden in old age. Some primitive tribes practice headhunting. In Saudi Arabia until this past year, women could not drive, and they still cannot leave their home unless accompanied by a husband, father, or brother. When my students say that we have no right to judge another culture, I then will raise a question that makes them think twice. What about slavery in the American south? What about Jim Crow laws after slavery was outlawed? Should these be outlawed, or are they simply part of the culture?

Does one culture ever have the right to judge another culture? Or are ethical laws simply cultural norms that vary from community to community? This was the opinion of the famed anthropologist Ruth Benedict (1887–1948), who taught that what we call ethics are simply cultural habits. Every culture has its own habits, and no culture has the right to judge another. For any culture to force its ethical ideas on another is a form of exploitation. The idea that ethics can vary by cultures is called cultural relativism.

The idea goes back to the ancient Greeks, and a group known as the Sophists. The Sophists were itinerant teachers who taught a kind of ethical relativism. One of their most famous spokesmen, Protagoras (487–412 BCE), famously said, "Man is the measure of all things." Ethics are manmade, with no universal ethical system by which to judge. In a sense, it is like modern attorneys who rather than search for truth, must learn to defend clients on either side of any issue. The Sophist point of view can easily lead to ethical subjectivism, where everyone decides ethics for themselves. It certainly leads to the kind of cultural relativism mentioned above.

Socrates strongly disagrees with the Sophists. He taught that there are absolute universal ethical statements, and through Socratic dialogue we can uncover these ethical statements. His student Plato taught that there is an eternal world of the forms, where such absolute ethical standards dwell. There is absolute justice, absolute charity, absolute piety, and absolute kindness. Socrates believed that we can discover these absolute ethical standards through dialogue with one another. One of the most fascinating questions of philosophy is whether Socrates and Plato are correct, can we discover some universal ethics which set the standard across all cultures? Or are the Sophists right, that ethics are manmade and can vary from culture to culture?

Let me say a word in favor of cultural relativism. Cultural relativists would teach that ethics are a social construct, manmade by every culture. Many sociologists think that there is a great deal of truth to this idea.

Austrian-born sociologist Peter Berger (b. 1929) taught that all human knowledge is in truth a social construct. Animals live in a world of nature. Humans, unlike animals, live in a world of culture. Culture is passed on by language. Berger, in a book he coauthored with Thomas Luckmann called *The Social Construction of Reality*, considered all human knowledge to be a social construct. To think about this, everything we humans consider important—from nations to money, from marriage to gender, from race to religion—exist because humans have chosen to understand the world this way. They do not exist in nature. They are simply part of how humans see the world.

Berger wrote another book called *The Sacred Canopy* about the social construction of religion, using the term *nomos* for its vision of reality, the truths every religion wants its adherents to accept. Such ideas as God, revelation, prayer, ritual, heaven, hell, and yes ethics, exist not in nature but rather in our shared cultural ideals. They are part of a sacred canopy we humans erect over our society. To Berger, religion may be important in helping a society understand itself, but that religion is not a true reflection of reality. Religion can change as circumstances change, and thus ethics can change.

If religion is a social construct, one can claim that ethics is also such a social construct. Different cultures create ethical laws to help provide some kind of structure and order. Such ethical laws have no reality in nature but are simply part of the way a culture views the world. For example, cultures throughout the world have developed a prohibition of incest, because sexual relations between relatives can undermine families, which are the basic building blocks of society. These ethical laws are not part of nature, with no ontological reality beyond the individual cultures that institutionalized them. Similarly, laws against murder, adultery, and stealing are part of a social construct, created by a particular culture to serve particular needs.

On a personal level, I am deeply troubled by this idea of ethics as a mere social construct: I cannot help but believe that ethics must be something more. The great Catholic theologian Thomas Aquinas, building on the work of Aristotle, taught that there a doctrine of natural law. Certain kinds of ethical behavior are part of nature rather than culture. They are built into the nature of the universe as much as gravity or electromagnetism. Laws against murder and stealing can be shown to be part of nature itself. Aquinas also taught that sexual intercourse must be performed naturally, with the purpose of procreation. This doctrine of natural law is the reason why the Catholic Church, following Aquinas, outlaws artificial contraception. Nonetheless, this positing of natural law, that ethics is not simply manmade, but built into the very structure of the universe, has a long history.

Let us now suppose that Aquinas and the natural law theorists are correct, that ethics are universal and built into the very structure of the universe. What is the source of these universal ethics? Aquinas would answer that God is the source, but this would bring us back to the problems discussed in divine command theory. Nonetheless, if religion is not the source of ethics and if culture is not the source of ethics, then what is? Let us explore two possibilities. Perhaps there is a scientific basis for ethics. This is at the heart of the ethical system called utilitarianism. Or perhaps human reason is the source of ethics. This is at the heart of the ethical system called deontology. Let us look at both possibilities in our quest to find a universal ethical system.

Science and Ethics

Let us turn to one of the fundamental branches of philosophy, known as epistemology. Epistemology is the study of knowledge—how do we know what we know? There are two major approaches to epistemology, rationalism and empiricism. In a nutshell, rationalism says that knowledge comes from the mind. We are born with certain innate knowledge, and we can uncover this knowledge through careful thought. Our senses can never be totally trusted. As Rene Descartes wrote in the early seventeenth century, there may be an evil demon who is tricking us. (If Descartes lived today, he would probably quote the movie *The Matrix*.) But our mind can be trusted to give us what philosophers call true, justified knowledge.

Philosophers such as Descartes, Spinoza, and Leibniz were all rationalists. But the root of rationalism goes back to Plato, who taught that our mind has knowledge we learned before we were born, when our souls existed in World of the Forms. Through careful rational thought we can uncover that knowledge.

The other major approach is empiricism, which says that knowledge comes from our senses. A simple summary of empiricism, often attributed to Aristotle, is "there is nothing in the mind that is not first in the senses." (I have never been able to find the original source of that quote, although it nicely summarizes Aristotle's view.) Aristotle rejected Plato's world of the forms and taught that there is only the empirical world we see with our senses. Later, John Locke would teach that our mind is a *tabula rasa*, a blank slate on which the world writes. There is no innate knowledge. Locke, Berkeley, and Hume were all empiricists.

In the next section we will look at ethics and rationalism. For now, let us study ethics and empiricism. Modern science is part of the empiricist tradition. It is based on observance of the universe, forming hypotheses, and testing those hypotheses with further observance. Science teaches that knowledge comes through our senses. Can science teach us about ethics? Can we learn right and wrong from observing the world?

To empiricist David Hume the answer is clear. He declared, "We cannot learn an ought from an is." We cannot look into the world, see what is out there, and then learn what we ought to do. Later thinkers would call this the naturalistic fallacy. We cannot learn ethics from nature. For example, the following statement is fallacious: "Obesity is rising among young people, therefore we should outlaw sodas in schools." The first half about obesity is an *is* statement, a fact about the world. The second half about outlawing sodas is an *ought* statement, a value. Perhaps there are good reasons to sell sodas in school, such as personal freedom, even if obesity is rising. To Hume, what we learn about the world can never be a source of ethical behavior.

So for Hume, what is the source of ethical behavior? Hume uses the term *sentiments*. They are mere feelings or sentiments. A later empiricist thinker, A. J. Ayer, taught an even more extreme kind of empiricism. To say that murder is wrong is the same as saying "murder, ugh, I don't like it." There is no real difference between saying, "I don't like murder" and saying, "I don't like strawberry ice cream." It is purely a matter of subjective feelings. As we learned in the introduction to this book, Ludwig Wittgenstein, teacher in a school known as logical positivism, said that we can only talk about two kinds of statements. We can talk about statements that are true by logic or definition. And we can talk about empirical statements, that can be verified by science. Every other kind of statement, including a statement about ethics, is simply nonsense. We cannot talk about it, and therefore it is best that we be silent. (Fortunately for Western philosophy, Wittgenstein rejected logical positivism later in life and came up with a new philosophy that permits us to speak about ethics. Wittgenstein's new philosophy is based on the idea of shared language.)

Should we give up on science as a source of ethics, on learning ethics by observing the world? Fortunately, there has been one brilliant attempt to develop a scientific ethical system, conceived by Jeremy Bentham (1748–1832) and further developed by his student and godson John Stuart Mill (1806–1873). The method is called utilitarianism. The basic idea behind utilitarianism is that all humans seek pleasure and avoid pain. We can measure the amount of pleasure and the amount of pain of any of our activities. In fact, Bentham developed an entire calculus to measure the relative pleasure and pain of various actions. According to utilitarianism, an act is ethical if it maximizes pleasure and minimizes pain.

Utilitarianism is a consequential approach to ethics. Activities are judged by their consequences. Nothing is good nor bad on its own; it is only good or bad based on the consequences. Does a particular act maximize pleasure and minimize pain? Murder is wrong because it causes pain not only to the victim but to the family. However, what if someone's murder would cause pleasure to many other people. In 2001 the disturbing movie *Bully* came out, based on the true story of the 1993 murder of teenager Bobby Kent in Fort Lauderdale. A group of fellow teens joined together to murder Kent because of his constant bullying of others. A utilitarian could argue that the murder was an ethical act because, by removing a bully, these teens creating more pleasure than pain. This is just an egregious example of where I believe utilitarian thinking goes wrong.

Still, utilitarian arguments are common today in discussing public policy. For example, is it ever permissible to torture someone to stop a terrorist act? Can we torture a person who might have knowledge of where a terrorist bomb was planted? Utilitarians would say yes, because the amount of pleasure from those saved from the act would far outweigh the pain of the person being tortured. But can we say torture is ethical?

There has been one modern attempt to use utilitarian-type arguments to build ethics on science, by an author who passionately rejects God and religion. Sam Harris has written a thoughtful book called *The Moral Landscape: How Science Can Determine Human Values.*[1] In his book, Harris says that science can measure human flourishing. Those activities which lead to human flourishing are precisely the activities that are ethical. Those activities that prevent human flourishing are precisely the activities that are not ethical. Therefore, we can learn ethics from science.

I enjoyed the book, partly because Harris is a charming and thoughtful writer. Nonetheless, there seemed to be a hole in his argument that I could not pin down. And then I realized: Harris based his book on the notion that the human flourishing is the basis of ethics. But where does this idea come from? Why is human flourishing important? Perhaps something else can be the basis of ethics. Modern science is built on the notion of evolution, that humans evolved through an ongoing struggle for survival. (I will have more to say about evolution later.) Maybe the ethical is whatever helps the survival of the fittest. Maybe it would be ethical to sterilize the mentally incompetent and make sure only the smartest had children. This was precisely what Justice Oliver Wendell Holmes Jr. wrote in the 1927 case of *Buck v. Bell*, "Three generations of imbeciles are enough." Was Holmes unethical? Something tells me that we need something more than utilitarianism on which

1. Harris, *Moral Landscape*.

to base our ethics. Perhaps we should follow the lead of the great Enlightenment philosopher Immanuel Kant (1724–1804), and turn to human reason.

Reason and Ethics

Although Kant lived before either Bentham or Mill, he totally rejected the thinking that went into their ethical system. He rejected any kind of consequential ethics. He called it the hypothetical imperative. For example, if someone says, "I will be honest in my business so that I will have a good reputation," they are not being ethical. They are simply acting in order to achieve a certain result. If someone says, "I will give charity because it makes me feel good," that is also not an ethical act. Something can only be ethical if done with no consideration of the consequences.

Kant taught what he called the categorical imperative. One has an ethical obligation to act in a certain way, with no regard for the consequences. "Be honest in business." "Give charity." "Thou shalt not murder." "Thou shalt not commit adultery." "Thou shalt not steal." These are all categorical imperatives. The Ten Commandments, with their categorical statements of right and wrong, are examples of Kant's ethical thinking. Kantian ethics is often termed deontological, based on the Latin word *deon*, for "duty." Unlike utilitarianism, deontological ethics are totally nonconsequential. One should act in a certain way, regardless of the consequences.

Deontological ethics are nonempirical. We do not learn how to act by exploring the outside world. Rather, we learn ethics through rational thought. Rationally, what is the best way to behave? Kant generalized his categorical imperative: "Act only according to that maxim whereby you can at the same time will that it should become a universal law." How would we want everyone to act? That should be the basis of our actions. For example, we would want it to be a universal law that everyone kept their promises. Therefore, we should always keep our promises.

Kant formulized other wordings of his categorical imperative. For example, he wrote that act in a way that treats people as ends in themselves, not simply as means. The important point for Kant is that consequences do not matter. The only thing that matters is whether we want something to be a universal law. It is an approach to ethics based on reason, what Kant called "practical reason." We can do right and wrong by searching our own mind.

Nonetheless, there is a serious problem with Kant's thinking. Do consequences truly not matter? One can argue that lying is always wrong. Rationally, we would want to live in a world where people do not lie, where we can trust people's words. However, if a family was hiding Jews in their

attic and Nazis came by asking if there were Jews, should they tell the truth
or lie? In this case Kant's thinking would lead to disastrous consequences.
There are times when lying is the ethical thing to do. And there are times
where breaking a promise is the ethical thing to do. One can even think of
a case where incest is the ethical thing to do. Picture the book of Genesis,
Lot and his daughters hiding in a cave thinking they are the last surviving
humans on earth. Both daughters sleep with their father to replenish the
earth. Is that unethical?

Kant goes wrong by thinking that ethics is absolute. He does not take
in special cases, where a more utilitarian approach might lead to a different decision. But there is a deeper problem with Kant's approach. Kant's
philosophy is totally secular. He believes that God was part of the noumenal
world that humans cannot know. He argues for his categorical imperative
on secular grounds. And that is where Kant gets into trouble.

At some point, there has to be a reason why we need to be good. Let
me quote what Alan L. Mittleman wrote about Kant:

> He [Kant] becomes the preeminent philosopher of human dig-
> nity and human rights. But his argument hangs, as it were, by
> a hair. It assumes a long Jewish and Christian prologue to the
> story of human worth, without, of course, invoking that back-
> story. Yet it is hard to see how Kant's endorsement of human
> worth, as edifying as it is, escapes circularity. If it does not, as I
> suspect, then arguments such as Kant's may need help from the
> very religious sources that they attempt to preempt.[2]

We have come full circle. We started by quoting Socrates, that ethics
must exist before God, and that God commanded us to be good because
that is ethical. We ended by quoting Kant, and realizing that Kant needs
to affirm human dignity as the foundation of his ethical system. Human
dignity is built on the fact that humans have some special ontological status,
that they are more than mere animals. Humans are worthy because God
said so.

All of this fits nicely with classical theism, and the belief that an all-
powerful God created humans in his image. But it is much harder to teach
such ideas in a materialist human view, when humans evolved from other
animals and are essentially no different from animals. Why should I treat
humans different from animals? Or the flip side of the question, already
raised by Peter Singer in his book on animal rights,[3] why should I not treat
animals exactly as humans, with the same rights? In part II of this book, we

2. Mittleman, *Human Nature*, 36.

3. Singer, *Animal Liberation*.

will tackle a second creation story, this one based on materialism. Finding a basis for ethics in a materialist world will become much harder.

PART II

The Second Creation Story
—Materialism

א בְּרֵאשִׁית בָּרָא אֱלֹהִים אֵת הַשָּׁמַיִם וְאֵת הָאָרֶץ: ב וְהָאָרֶץ הָיְתָה תֹהוּ וָבֹהוּ
וְחֹשֶׁךְ עַל־פְּנֵי תְהוֹם וְרוּחַ אֱלֹהִים מְרַחֶפֶת עַל־פְּנֵי הַמָּיִם: ג וַיֹּאמֶר אֱלֹהִים יְהִי־אוֹר
וַיְהִי־אוֹר: ד וַיַּרְא אֱלֹהִים אֶת־הָאוֹר כִּי־טוֹב וַיַּבְדֵּל אֱלֹהִים בֵּין הָאוֹר וּבֵין הַחֹשֶׁךְ:
ה וַיִּקְרָא אֱלֹהִים | לָאוֹר יוֹם וְלַחֹשֶׁךְ קָרָא לָיְלָה וַיְהִי־עֶרֶב וַיְהִי־בֹקֶר יוֹם אֶחָד:

"At the beginning of God's creation of the heaven and the earth, when the
earth was without form, and void; and darkness was upon the face of the deep,
and the Spirit of God hovered upon the face of the water, God said, Let there
be light: and there was light. And God saw the light, that it was good: and God
divided the light from the darkness. And God called the light Day, and the
darkness he called Night. And there was chaos and there was order, one day."

(Genesis 1:1–5)

69

CHAPTER 5

Materialism—What If Everything Is Matter?

When the French mathematician and astronomer Simon-Pierre Marquis de Laplace (1749–1827) wrote his classic work Celestial Mechanics, he presented a copy to the emperor Napoleon. Napoleon looked through the book and commented, "I see no mention of God in this book." Laplace responded, "I have no need for such a hypothesis." Laplace went on to say, imagine a powerful demon that had a complete knowledge of the location and the momentum of every particle of the universe. With such information, this demon could predict the entire future and retrodict the entire past of the universe.

Since I was in high school I have been thinking about entropy, the idea that all physical systems, including the universe, must run down over time. That was where I first read the story "The Last Question" by Isaac Asimov, in his book *Nine Tomorrows*.[1] Asimov considered this his greatest short story. I must agree, seeing that have been obsessed by this story for over fifty years.

Spoiler Alert: I am going to give away the ending of the story in this paragraph. The story takes place at various times in the future when a computer of greater and greater complexity is asked the question, how can we

1. Asimov, "Last Question." The story was originally published in the November 1956 issue of *Science Fiction* and his been reprinted many times.

stop the entropy of the universe? The computer always answers that there is insufficient data. As the story advantages, the computer itself becomes self-creating, forming newer versions of itself. It stops being something physical and eventually becomes an energy field. But there is still insufficient data. Finally, after humans have ceased to have bodies and become part of this one universal mind, the last stars are disappearing, and the end of the universe is at hand. The computer, which now encompasses a kind of universal mind, is still working on this problem. At last it comes up with an answer how to stop the entropy of the universe: "Let there be light."

Primordial Matter

We turn now to our second creation story. If the first story was about God creating an entire universe from nothing (*creation ex nihilo*), this story is much simpler. Creation is about making order out of chaos. Primordial matter exists, but it exists in a chaotic state. God's creative activity is simply to move that matter toward greater and greater order.

Most biblical scholars believe that the movement from chaos to order was the actual intention of the original biblical author. There was a primordial water, a kind of primitive matter that existed before creation. God moves that water from chaos to order through various acts of separation and distinction. This image of God bringing the chaotic water under control appears not only in Genesis but in numerous other places in the Bible. For example, in the book of Job, God speaks to the oceans of the world with these words, "Thus far shall you come, but no further; and here shall your proud waves be stayed" (Job 38:11). God tames the waters, bringing the wildness of water under control. This idea also appears in the book of Psalms: "You rule the raging of the sea; when its waves arise, you still them" (Psalms 89:10). In the Noah story, God removes the separation between the upper waters and the lower waters, allowing chaos to reign once again.

If the waters preexisted creation, what is the proper translation of the first verse in Genesis? The translation, "In the beginning God created the heaven and the earth," is extremely problematic, not fitting the Hebrew. Rashi, the great biblical commentary, already says about this verse: "the verse cries out, interpret me!" Let us look carefully at the Hebrew of this verse. The first word, *bereshit*, means "in the beginning of." The word *bereishit* must be followed by another noun—in the beginning of something. (This is known as a *smikhut*, a common Hebrew form that joins two nouns together, for example, "bar mitzvah," "Rosh Hashanah," "Simchat Torah.") The second word, *bara*, is a verb "created." This would make the first two words of Genesis, "in the beginning of created," a phrase that makes no sense. The logical meaning of the verse is in the beginning of the creation. That is why I translated the verse above, "at the beginning of God's creation of the heaven and the earth." And that is why the Jewish Publication Society translates the verse, "When God began to create the heaven and the earth."

According to this translation, the first act of God is when He says, "let there be light." But before the creation of light there is a primordial water. The water stands for a primordial stuff, something that existed before God takes any action. Where did this water, this primordial stuff, come from? Plato, in his creation story *The Timaeus*, sees a demigod, a lesser god, creating the world out of such primordial stuff. This matter always existed. But of course, the Greeks thought the universe was eternal, having no beginning. How did Jewish tradition understand this act? Let us look at one of the great biblical commentators, known for his mystical bent, Nachmanides or the Ramban (1194–1270):

> Now listen to the correct and clear explanation of the verse at its simplest. The Holy One, blessed be He, created all things from absolute non-existence. Now we have no expression in the sacred language for bringing forth something from nothing other than the verb *bara* (created). Nonetheless, everything that exists under the sun or above was not made from non-existence at the outset. Instead He brought forth from total and absolute nothing a very thin substance devoid of corporeality but having a power of potency, fit to assume form and to proceed from potentiality to reality. This was the primary matter created by God; it is called by the Greeks *hyle* (matter.) After the *hyle*, He did not create anything, but He formed and made things with it, and from this *hyle*. He brought everything into existence and clothed it with forms and put them into their final condition.

What Ramban is saying is that God created primordial matter from nothing. This primordial matter was without form and was used to create everything in the universe. (Note: Aristotle would disagree, saying that you cannot have matter without form. Plato, on the other hand, would see this primordial matter as the fundamental stuff of the universe.) Ramban would go on to say that this fundamental matter was the *tohu*, the first half of the phrase *tohu v'vohu* (void and without form). *Tohu* stands for "matter" and *vohu* stands for "form." Later the *Zohar*, the great thirteenth-century work of Jewish mysticism, would say the same thing, *tohu* or primordial matter came first, and then was given *vohu* form.[2]

2. *Zohar* I 16a.

Ramban, in keeping with Plato, seems to be saying that there is a kind of primordial matter, unformed, and the creation of the universe was accomplished through giving form to this primordial matter. Plato said that matter always existed. Ramban said that God's only act of creation from nothing was making that matter. The Bible, when it says that "hovered upon the face of the water," uses the term *water* for this primordial matter. Modern science will also claim that there was primordial matter, but it came about not through an act of God, but through a big bang. The world is made of unformed matter, going through a process of formation. This is the basic idea behind materialism.

What Is Materialism?

In Part I, we looked at dualism, the idea that there are two substances that make up the universe: matter and spirit or body and soul. In Part II we are going to look at a form of monism known as materialism, that there is only one substance that makes up the universe, and this substance is matter. In Part III we are going to look at an alternate form of monism known as idealism, that there is only one substance that makes up the universe and that is mind. But for now, let us assume that everything is matter; only matter exists and nothing else. Materialism is also often known as physicalism—everything is physical; science, in studying the physical world, can explain everything.

Most scientists today are materialists or physicalists. They believe their calling is to study the physical stuff of the universe—atoms, molecules, cells, tissues, physical objects, and physical systems. They assume that there is no spiritual reality that can interact with the physical. The universe of the physical is a totally closed system; there is no room for a God who exists outside the system and who interacts with the physical. Recall in our chapter on dualism that the interaction between mind and matter was an extremely difficult, ultimately unanswerable issue. The simple scientific solution is that only matter in motion exists. Many contemporary philosophers follow this scientific reasoning, interpreting the world in strictly materialist terms.

The beginning of materialism occurred in ancient Greece, where the philosopher Democritus (460–370 BCE) taught that everything in the universe is made up of atoms, tiny substances that cannot be further divided. He believed these atoms function by natural laws, rather than the final causes as Aristotle would later teach. Today, scientists follow in Democritus's footsteps, seeing atoms as the ultimate building blocks of everything. Of course, today we know that atoms can further be divided. They are made of electrons whirling around a nucleus of protons and neutrons, which are themselves made of quarks. Modern physicists speak of an entire particle zoo. Nonetheless, modern physics is built on Democritus's ideas. Quantum mechanics does raise problems for Democritus's view; we will explore this later in this book.

This atomist theory of Democritus became a fundamental part of Epicurean philosophy. The poet Lucretius (99–55 BCE) introduced these Epicurean ideas to a Roman audience in his epic poem *De Rerum Natura*—"On the Nature of Things." To Lucretius, the physical world functions not by interference by the gods or eternal beings, but through atoms that act by natural laws. These atoms sometimes "swerve" from their natural paths, causing the objects of the world to form and function. Stephen Greenblatt describes this in his Pulitzer Prize–winning book on Lucretius: "The stuff of the universe, Lucretius proposed, is an infinite number of atoms moving randomly through space like dust motes in a sunbeam, colliding, hooking together, forming complex structures, breaking apart again, in a ceaseless process of creation and destruction."[3] It is a world made of stuff.

A key part of this materialist worldview is that this fundamental stuff, these atoms, have no subjective awareness. They are blind. In a sense they are like billiard balls on a table reacting to the cue stick and each other, but with no awareness of their own. They have no inner desires or drives, a sharp break with Aristotle's teaching that every particle has a telos or purpose. The entire project of science is to study the movements of this material stuff, attempting to give a mathematical account of their actions. Later Galileo would famously teach that "mathematics is the language of the universe."

These ancient Greek ideas became part of modern thinking in the later Renaissance. Thomas Hobbes (1588–1679), who developed the theory of social contract, was a materialist. He spoke of the need for a strong government that he called the *Leviathan*, in order to bring human nature under control. Without such a government, life would be "solitary, poor, nasty, brutish, and short."[4] Humans were driven by material forces causing them to do evil, unless the fear of the state could control them. Similarly, Pierre-Simon Laplace, quoted at the beginning of this chapter, was a materialist. Laplace's famous demon became the ultimate example of not simply materialism but determinism, the idea that every event in the universe has a previous cause, and these causes totally determine the future. The problem with determinism is that it denies the possibility of free will, a problem we will tackle later.

3. Greenblatt, *Swerve*, 5.
4. Hobbes, Leviathan, 78.

Perhaps the most influential modern materialist was Karl Marx, who taught that economic forces are the cause of everything. He called his philosophy dialectic materialism, building on Hegel's dialectic but giving it a material cause. (Hegel was an idealistic who taught that everything is mind, and that mind functions in history through a series of stages known as thesis, antithesis, and synthesis. Hegel called this the dialectic. Marx said that he was turning Hegel on his head, claiming that the dialectic was not something in the world of mind—idealism, but rather in the world of matter or economics—materialism.)

Most modern scientists and philosophers, with some prominent exceptions, see the world in purely materialistic terms. Everything is matter in motion. Matter moves by natural laws, perhaps established by God at the moment of creation. In the Enlightenment period many of these philosophers and scientists were deists, believing that God set the world in motion but does not intervene. To such deists as Thomas Jefferson, the world is a kind of perpetual motion machine, set in motion by God who no longer intercedes. Eventually deism gave way to atheism. It was not God but the big bang, a natural event, that set the machine in motion. Many modern scientists and philosophers, but certainly not all, are atheists. When asked about God, like Laplace they claim that they have no need for such a hypothesis. The rules of the universe are simply brute facts. To study the world is to study matter in motion. Matter is all that exists.

Nonetheless, this materialism is going to raise some serious issues we will explore throughout the section. The first is hinted at by our interpretation of the creation story. How can the universe go from chaos to order, when entropy teaches that the universe should go from order to chaos?

Chaos to Order

The biblical creation story is a description of going from chaos to order. At the beginnings of creation are the chaotic waters, which God separates on the second day into the upper and lower waters. Later rabbinic tradition would note that the second day is the only one where the Torah never says, "God saw that it was good." Separation was necessary for creation to go forward, but such separation is touched with sadness. According to the midrash, the upper waters and the lower waters cried out for one another.[5] Recall what we wrote in the chapter about evil when we looked at the work of Marcelo Gleiser. He wrote that the universe is broken, and that very

---

5. *Genesis Rabbah* 13:13.

brokenness allows it to move forward. Gleiser sees a universe in process. But process must begin with pain.

Separations lead to daily acts of creation that seem to follow an almost evolutionary pattern. On the third day God creates plants, on the fourth day the heavenly bodies, on the fifth day lower animals, on the sixth day mammals, and eventually humanity. The movement is toward greater and greater order. But perhaps there is hint in the classical phrase used at the end of each day of creation, *vihee erev vihee boker*—"there was evening and there was morning." What do the Hebrew words *erev* and *boker* really mean?

The word *erev* means "evening." But it actually comes from Hebrew meaning "mixed up, indistinct." In the evening we cannot see things clearly; everything is mixed up. This meaning can be seen in other places. For example, Orthodox Jews will often build an *eruv*, a boundary allowing people to carry or push baby carriages in public places on Shabbat. But the *eruv* developed in Talmudic times with the tradition of a number of households mixing food together, making their shared courtyard into one private area rather than a public area. Carrying is then permitted in such a private area. Similarly, the fourth of the plagues that descended on Egypt is *erov*. The words mean a mixture of something, interpreted as everything from a mixture of insects to wild animals.

The word *boker* literally comes from a root meaning to make distinct. At the end of the book of Leviticus, we learn that the Priest, in looking at certain offerings, shall not distinguish between good and bad—*lo livaker ben tov lera* (Leviticus 27:33). The root actually means to search in order to make distinctions. We can understand the words "there was evening and there was morning" to mean "there was confusion and there was distinction." Or as I rather provocatively translated it above, "there was chaos and there was order." The second creation story is an account of moving from chaos to order.

In a sense, this movement from chaos to order is precisely the story told by modern cosmologists. In the beginning, which means immediately after the big bang, there was a chaotic, high-energy mix of particles, quarks, and leptons, often called a plasma. There was no visible light, but only electromagnetic radiation at the highest energy level, what we call gamma rays. This energy prevented these early particles from coalescing into atoms. If quarks came together to form a proton and an electron joined it, a photon of electromagnetic energy would knock it out of place. Only as the universe expanded did the universe begin to cool, allowing the first atoms to be formed. For the first time electromagnetic waves also became less energetic, going from gamma rays to X-rays to ultraviolet rays and finally to visible light. Visible that is, if there was anyone to see it. The biblical phrase "let there be light" could not have happened until the universe began to cool off.

Finally, in this cooler universe, single protons and electrons joined together to form hydrogen atoms. Gravity caused these hydrogen atoms to clump together, beginning a process of nuclear fusion, turning hydrogen into helium, and letting off energy. Stars were born. Stars give off energy the same way as hydrogen bombs, through the nuclear fusion of hydrogen into helium. The universe was moving from pure chaos to greater and greater distinction. Eventually these primitive stars would explode, creating higher elements, particularly carbon and oxygen to form.

The carbon and other higher elements formed a kind of space dust that eventually coalesced around certain stars. In particular, this dust formed planets around a relatively average star in a relatively average galaxy called the Milky Way. One of those planets was exactly the right distance from the sun for a chemical with two hydrogen and one oxygen atom—water—to remain in liquid form. Water remains liquid in only a small temperature range. If the earth were a bit closer to the sun (turning the water to steam), or a bit farther from the sun (turning the water to ice), life would never have evolved. Life is dependent on the unique chemical properties of liquid water.

On earth, we have a movement toward greater and greater order. Carbon atoms, made up of six protons and able to join other carbon atoms, began to form long chains. The details of these carbon compounds are in any organic chemistry textbook. The important point is that long strings of molecules became proteins and eventually a self-replicating molecule called DNA. So life began. At first life was simple, one-celled creatures, prokaryotes, and then slightly more complex eukaryotes. Eventually multicellular creatures appeared, and cell differentiation began. In multicelled creatures including human beings, stem cells would branch out and specialize, becoming nerves or muscles, blood or bone. Evolution is the process by which biological diversity spread across the planet known as Earth. We will deal in the next chapter with the religious issues raised by evolution. But scientists have painted a vision of the world similar to the biblical vision, a universe going from chaos to order.

This image does raise a difficulty. How does this movement from chaos to order fit in with the law of entropy, which teaches that a closed system will always move from order to chaos? This requires further exploration.

Two Laws of Thermodynamics

The biblical picture of creation from chaos to order pictures God intervening each step of the way. God separates the upper and lower waters, God
creates the plants and then the animals, and finally God creates humanity.
The scientific picture of creation from chaos to order sees the process as
happening naturally, some would say by blind chance, without any divine
intervention. Such a view is based on the notion that the universe is a closed
system, behaving according to its own rules without room for intervention
from outside the system.

To understand the problem this raises, let us turn to the two laws of
thermodynamics. The first law teaches that energy cannot be created or
destroyed within a closed system. Today, since Einstein proved the equivalence of matter and energy, we can reword this that matter-energy cannot
be created nor destroyed within a closed system. If the entire universe is a
closed system, then it contains a fixed amount of mass-energy, which can
be transformed into various forms. Energy can be changed into matter and
matter can be changed into energy. The form of energy can change. But no
energy can be added from the outside.

Let us suppose that a supernatural agent intervenes with the universe
from the outside. This would add energy to the system, contradicting the
idea of the first law of thermodynamics. So it seems that this would prevent
any kind of divine intervention, even some kind of partial providence. The
religious philosopher Alfred Plantiga has offered a solution. He claims that
the universe is not a closed system, but rather God is part of the system. God
is allowed to intervene. To quote Plantiga:

> According to Newton and classical mechanics, natural laws de-
> scribe how the world works when, or provided that the world
> is a closed (isolated) system, subject to no outside causal influ-
> ence. In classical physics, the great conservation laws deduced
> from Newton's laws are stated for closed or isolated systems.
> These principles, therefore, apply to isolated or closed systems.
> If so, however, there is nothing in them to prevent God from
> changing the velocity or direction of a particle. If he did so, ob-
> viously, energy would not be conserved in the system in ques-
> tion; but equally obviously, that system would not be closed, in
> which case the principle of conservation of energy would not
> apply to it.[6]

6. Plantinga, *Where the Conflict*, 78.

Plantiga claims that the idea that the universe is a closed system is not a scientific statement but rather a theological one. It is a way of closing out religion or any reference to God or divine providence. With great respect for his argument, we are assuming a materialist view of reality in this section. For our purposes we must leave God out, and see a universe closed, made of material stuff that obeys the conservation laws of energy.

The second law of thermodynamics is a greater concern when considering the movement from chaos to order. This is the law of entropy, the measure of randomness and chaos. The law teaches that in any closed system, over time, the amount of entropy or randomness will increase. When I teach this, I tell my students to imagine a teenager's room. Unless they put energy into it and clean it up, over time it will become messier and messier, more chaotic. To give an example I once heard from another rabbi, imagine a brand-new car abandoned in the forest for two hundred years. At the end of that time there will be a pile of rusted metal, rubber, and plastic. Leave a pile of rusted metal, rubber, and plastic in the wilderness for two hundred years, there will never be a brand-new car.

Entropy is an inexorable law of the universe. Everything breaks down over time, even our bodies, even the sun, even the universe itself. To quote the poet W. B. Yeats in my favorite poem, *The Second Coming*, written after World War I: "Things fall apart, the centre cannot hold." Hot coffee left out will reach room temperature, and the ice in a drink will melt. You can scramble an egg but you cannot unscramble it. Everything moves toward greater randomness. Yet we just described how life evolved on earth, in a movement toward greater and greater order. Evolution appears to be anti-entropy.

Materialists do have an answer. They claim that the entropy of an entire system always increases. The earth appears to moving in an anti-entropy direction, toward greater order, because it receives energy from the sun. But as hydrogen turns to helium in the sun, entropy increases. The total entropy of the system, earth plus sun, is increasing, even as life evolves on earth. So the second law of thermodynamics is not broken. Yet why would the universe be built in such a way that one little planet would go from chaos to order, that entropy would decrease on earth. If we remove God from the equation and assume that the universe is a closed system, it is problematic.

One Somewhat Radical Solution

Where do we stand? According to materialism, we have a universe filled with tiny bits of matter that behave according to scientific laws. These bits of matter have no subjectivity, they neither see nor feel, but remain totally passive while they are acted on by outside forces. That universe is a closed system. According to the first law of thermodynamics, no energy can be added to or subtracted from the system. This means that we cannot have a supernatural entity, God or anything else, which manipulates these particles from outside the system. Materialists must reject divine providence.

According to the second law of thermodynamics, entropy must always increase. This closed universe must go from greater order to greater chaos over time. This is true for the universe as a whole. But in certain places, particularly on our planet, the universe appears to be going from chaos to order. There is a movement toward greater and greater organization, away from chaos. How can this be? Perhaps we need to modify one of our fundamental ideas. Perhaps we ought to consider the possibility that this matter that makes up the universe is not utterly passive and blind, but contains some low level of consciousness. Perhaps we ought to consider the philosophical approach with a long history, but rejected by most modern philosophers, of panpsychism. Panpsychism teaches that mind is a fundamental feature of the universe. Mind is fundamental and all matter contains some low level of mind or consciousness.

Nobel Prize–winning chemist Ilya Prigogine already hints at this idea. He suggests that we ought to rethink how we understand chemistry, particularly when speaking of molecules that are in a state he calls far from equilibrium. He writes about how order arises among such molecules:

> We can speak of a new coherence, of a mechanism of `communication' among molecules. But this type of communication can arise only in far-from-equilibrium conditions. It is quite interesting that such communication seems to be the rule in the world of biology. It may in fact be taken as the very basis of the definition of biological systems.[7]

Prigogine indicates that these pieces of matter seems to communicate with each other, and this leads them to move toward greater order. They are not utterly passive. In fact, he continues, "To use somewhat anthropomorphic language: in equilibrium matter is 'blind,' but in far-from equilibrium conditions it begins to be able to perceive, to 'take into account,' in its way of functioning, differences in the eternal world."[8] Prigogine would probably deny that he is a panpsychist. But his thinking about how matter behaves certainly seems to point in that direction.

7. Prigogine and Stengers, *Order Out of Chaos*, 13.
8. Prigogine and Stengers, *Order Out of Chaos*, 14.

Prigogine's major goal is give a temporal understanding of reality. The laws of physics as enumerated by Newton can work equally well forward and backward. But reality seems to be moving in a certain direction. We can crack an egg and scramble it, but we cannot take scrambled eggs and unscramble them. So it is with many of the chemical reactions that make up our universe, they move in a particular direction. Particularly in biology such a temporal order exists. Embryos grow and develop, and the molecules that make up these embryos seem to understand what is expected of them. There seems to be an inner understanding among the particles that make up the universe that there is the direction they need to move in.

For Prigogine, it is not an external force that drives matter to self-organize. No God is manipulating matter. The universe is built on the idea of being and becoming, and the becoming seems to be inherent within matter itself. These ideas will be vital later in this book when we look at Alfred North Whitehead's process philosophy. But for the moment, let us turn from a chemist to a philosopher of mind, the Australian thinker David J. Chalmers.

Chalmers raised the question of the hard problem of consciousness. What does it mean to feel consciousness, the subjectivity that causes an awareness of pain, of color, of taste, of sound? Chalmers builds on the work of Thomas Nagel, who wrote a famous essay on the topic, "What is it like to be a bat?" What is actually going on in a bat's head as it uses sonar to navigate through the air? We humans can never know, for we are not bats. But we have something called consciousness that makes us aware. We know what it is to be a human. Could a computer ever simulate what it is to be a human?

Chalmers discusses a question we brought up earlier in this book. At what level of being does consciousness enter the universe? Does matter require a certain level of self-organization before we call it conscious? Are only humans conscious, as Descartes thought? What about dogs? Birds? Lizards? Insects? Amoebas? Chalmers believed that we cannot say consciousness begins at some level of organization but no lower. Like the joke about the turtles, "madam, it is turtles all the way down," so it is with consciousness. He believed it was consciousness all the way down. Consciousness is a fundamental property of the universe, like matter and energy.

Consciousness is fundamental to matter. To quote Chalmers:

> The view that there is experience wherever there is causal interaction is counterintuitive. But it is a view that can grow surprisingly satisfying with reflection, making consciousness better integrated into the natural order. It the view is correct,

consciousness does not come in sudden jagged spikes, with isolated complex systems arbitrarily producing rich conscious experiences. Rather, it is more uniform property of the universe, with very simple systems having very simple phenomenology, and complex systems having complex phenomenology. This makes consciousness less "special" in some ways, and so more reasonable.[9]

In fairness, Chalmers does not like the word panpsychism. He considered himself a dualist, there being two aspects of reality—matter and mind. But he also considered himself a naturalist, seeing the mind as a fundamental aspect of the universe that permeates everything from the simplest atoms to complicated animals. Science must study consciousness as a fundamental part of nature, just as they study mass and energy as fundamental parts of nature.

Let us suppose the materialists are right, matter is all that exists. But let us also suppose that those bits of matter have subjectivity, they are not simply blind bits of stuff moving by outside forces. In a sense, this is exactly what Aristotle said long ago—everything has a final cause or purpose, a direction it is trying to go. Scientists dismissed Aristotle at the end of the Renaissance period. But perhaps that dismissal was a bit hasty. Maybe there is room for a mind, and final causation in a material world.

Nowhere is this idea that matter seems to be moving in a direction, toward some goal, more prevalent than in the theory of evolution through natural selection. Many call evolution a blind process. In my mind, it is not blind at all, but proof that the natural world seems to moving toward something. In the next chapter we will tackle the controversial issue of evolution.

9. Chalmers, *Conscious Mind*, 298.

CHAPTER 6

Evolution—Must We Choose Between Moses and Darwin?

The little boy asked his mother, "where did human beings come from?" The mother responded, "God took the dust of the earth and formed it into a man, then breathed into the man the breath of God. God made both men and women in his image, just as the Bible says." The boy then said, "Daddy gave me a different answer. He said that we came from lower forms of animals, and we are direct descendants of apes." The mother answered, "He is talking about his side of the family. I am talking about my side of the family."

Our local Hebrew Day School high school invited me to give a talk to their Advanced Placement biology class. The students suffered from a certain cognitive dissonance. As a top academic school, the students in this biology class learned about evolution by natural selection in some detail. But the Jewish teachers at the school were very Orthodox rabbis who could not accept evolution for religious reasons. I came in to try to present a point of view that accepted the best of scientific knowledge with an acceptance of religious faith. I wanted to teach that one can be a believing Jew who accepts evolution. In fact, I took it a step further. I tried to show the class that the process of evolution actually points to the existence of God.

Design in the World

There is a popular idea out there that one must make a choice in life. One can believe in Darwin or one can believe in God. One can believe in science or one can believe in religion. This dichotomy is often exacerbated by passionate arguments on both sides. Religious fundamentalists will reject evolution and insist on the teaching of creation science, or at least some form of intelligent design, in the public schools. In response, ardent atheists will argue that there is no God but that biological development and diversity is totally the result of natural processes. This argument was the subject of the famous Scopes monkey trial in 1925, which pit Clarence Darrow arguing for evolution against William Jennings Brian arguing for the Bible. The trial became the basis of the stage play and movie *Inherit the Wind*.

So, who is correct in this argument of Moses versus Darwin? Where do I stand on this issue? As a rabbi, I accept the existence of God who created the world, with the understanding that there are a variety of interpretations about of the creation story. One of those interpretations is that God used evolution by natural selection to make a world. Some call this theistic evolution. As a scientifically oriented individual, I accept Darwin's theory as the best explanation of biological variety on earth. I see natural selection as the basis for design in this world. I believe in both the Bible and Darwin. As mentioned above, I will try to show in this chapter, more than disproving God, I believe evolution points toward God. After all, evolution is the most obvious example on earth of the movement from chaos to order, from lower to higher, more complicated forms of life. According to our understanding of Genesis, this is exactly how God created the world, moving matter from chaos to order.

I hope to show that evolution points toward the existence of God. But before I begin that quest, I need to discuss the entire issue of design in the world. One of the classic proofs for the existence of God is called the teleological proof. *Telos* means "purpose," and this proof shows that the universe seems to show purpose or design. The world seems to work by laws that point toward a designer, an intelligence that causes it to function the way it does. Of course, many modern scientists reject any such purpose or design in the universe. The Nobel Laureate Steven Weinberg famously wrote, "The more the universe seems comprehensible, the more it also seems pointless."[1]

Thomas Aquinas (1225–1274) in his *Summa Theologica*, brings his five proofs for the existence of God. Most of these fall under the category cosmological proofs, based on the fact that a chain of causes must have a first

---

1. Weinberg, *First Three Minutes*, 154.

cause. But his fifth proof is based on teleology, the presence of design in the world. If the world is designed, it must have a designer. The presumption is that the designer must be God. Of course, a simple refutation of the proof is that, even if there is a designer, the designer need not be God. Gnosticism, considered a heresy by the early Catholic Church, saw the designer as some lesser being, which they call a demiurge. This idea follows Plato, who in his dialog the *Timaeus* also speaks of a demiurge who was the designer of the universe.

Whatever its problems, the idea of design is the most popular argument used by defenders of religion to argue for the existence of God. I myself have expressed my belief to my congregation that I cannot imagine we are here by random chance, atoms crashing together in the right way. There must be a designer. Perhaps the most famous articulation of this idea comes from the eighteenth-century naturalist and clergyman William Paley (1743–1805). Paley writes that readers should imagine that they are walking on the beach and see a stone. They can assume the stone came about by natural causes. But on the other hand, suppose they were walking on the beach and saw a watch (in Paley's day it would be a pocket watch). Could you possibly imagine the watch is there by random chance? It seems to exist in order to fulfill a purpose, tell time. Its moving parts are correlated precisely in a way to allow it work correctly. One would have to assume that the watch must have a designer.

To quote Paley, "the inference we think is inevitable, that the watch must have had a maker—that here must have existed, at some time and at some place or other, an artificer or artificers, who formed it for the purpose which we found it."[2] Paley may be quoted by believers, but atheists also use his example to defend the lack of design in the universe. The best example is the passionate atheist Richard Dawkins (b. 1941), who called his book on evolution *The Blind Watchmaker*. To quote Dawkins:

> A true watchmaker has foresight: he designs his cogs and springs, and he plans their interconnections, with a future pur-
> pose in his mind's eye. Natural selection, the blind, unconscious automatic process which Darwin discovered, and which we now know is the explanation for the existence and apparently purposeful form of all life, has no purpose in mind. It has no mind and no mind's eye. It does not plan for the future. It has no vision, no foresight, no sight at all. If it can be said to play the role of watchmaker in nature, it is the blind watchmaker.[3]

2. Paley, *Natural Theology*, 10.

3. Dawkins, *Blind Watchmaker*, 9.

In this chapter we will explore whether evolution is truly a blind process, as asserted by Dawkins and others, or is there a teleology, as asserted by Paley.

Materialists such as Dawkins would assert that the process is blind, with no purpose. To quote him once again, "Evolution has no long-term goal. There is no long-distance target, no final perfection to serve as a criterion for selection, although human vanity cherishes the absurd notion that our species is the final goal of evolution."[4] Evolution happens by random chance with no ultimate direction or purpose. Another leading scientist of evolutionary theory, Stephen Jay Gould (1941–2002) has said that if evolution were to start over again, it would go in a totally different direction, not leading toward human beings. Again there is no direction, no purpose, no design, and no designer. It is all random chance.

So is Paley right? Is there design in the universe? And is that design a deliberate, intelligent process? Or is Dawkins right, was the universe designed by a blind watchmaker? Is there no purpose and no direction as stated by Weinberg? To partially answer that question, we must raise an issue we studied in the chapter on evil. If there is a designer, could he not have done a better job? There is the story of the man who goes to a tailor to have a suit made. He comes back a week later to pick up his suit, and the tailor says it is not ready. The man gets upset. "It has been a week. God made the universe in just six days." The tailor replies, "That may be true, but look at the universe and look at my suit." Or as I wrote in the chapter on evil, couldn't a designer God have made a better knee?

In the chapter on evil, I gave the example of a hospital that grew organically, building being added to building. Such organic growth seems true for all life. Let me give another example. Recently my son had his wisdom teeth pulled. Why do wisdom teeth become impacted, forcing so many people to have them removed? At one point in history early human ancestors, various primates, had large jaws. These jaws contained thirty-two teeth. But as primates evolved into humans, they grew bigger heads to hold larger brains. The brains were bigger, but the head must still pass through the birth canal of the mother. Giving birth is far more dangerous for humans, both for the mother and the baby, because of our large heads. To make some more room, our jaws became smaller. But we still had the same thirty-two teeth as our primate ancestors. The result is what keeps oral surgeons in business.

Paley is correct that there is design in the world. But the design is not necessarily a theistic God. Rather, the design itself is a natural process that follows certain scientific laws. This was the great insight of Charles Darwin (1809–1882), as well as his younger contemporary British naturalist Alfred

4. Dawkins, *Blind Watchmaker*, 9.

Russel Wallace (1823–1913). What is this process called natural selection? And is it truly blind, as materialists like Dawkins and Gould assert?

Evolution through Natural Selection

There is a prevalent idea that Darwin conceived the theory of evolution, that various forms of life change over time, and that different life forms have a common ancestor. This is untrue. Evolution was a well-established idea long before Darwin. In fact, Darwin's grandfather Erasmus Darwin (1731–1802) spoke of the relatedness of all forms of life. The idea that life forms are related and change over time is not a particularly religious problem, unless one reads the Bible in the most fundamentalist way. The Bible says that God made various forms of life "after its own kind." But each of these kinds of life can evolve and change over time.

Perhaps the most influential theoretician of such evolution was the French naturalist Jean-Baptiste Lamarck (1744–1822), founder of what is often called Lamarckian evolution. Lamarck taught that the offspring of organisms can directly be affected by the activities of their progenitors. Why do giraffes have long necks? Some giraffes would stretch out their necks to eat food higher up on the tree. Their offspring would have slightly longer necks, whose offspring would be longer still. Actions affect children, causing changes over the course of generations. Today, most mainstream biologists discredit Lamarckian evolution. But ideas that die out in one generation are sometimes revived in another generation. The field of epigenetics has created a new interest in Lamarck's ideas, as we will show later.

Darwin accepted the evolutionary theories of his grandfather and others. He developed a great insight, developed during the five years (1831–1836) he traveled around the world on the *HMS Beagle* as the ship naturalist. This insight, adaption through natural selection, revolutionized the way we see life on earth and became the foundation of any study of biology to our present day. Let me present a brief summary of Darwin's theory, before we tackle the question of whether this is truly a blind process.

Darwin, during his travels on the *Beagle*, was influenced by the work of Thomas Robert Malthus (1776–1834). Malthus had taught that the population will always grow at a faster rate than the food supply. As a result, in any population there will be a struggle for food. Those who are most fit will succeed at feeding themselves and surviving. Most will die off. With Malthus, we have a first example of survival of the fittest.

Darwin applied these ideas to all biological species. Over the course of generations, there will be small changes in some of the offspring of plants or animals. Most of those changes are negative and the offspring will not survive. But occasionally a change will be positive, giving the new generation a survival advantage over those without the change. These species will pass on these biological changes, and because they have a better chance of survival, they will flourish while those without the change will die off. Selection is dependent not only on small biological changes, but on the ability of a species to pass those changes on to a new generation.

A classic example mentioned by Darwin is the finches on the Galapagos Islands. Finches are small birds that descended from a common ancestor before the islands separated from one another. Darwin noticed that the food sources for these finches varied from island to island. As a result, the shape of the birds' beaks also varied from island to island. The finches that survived on each island and went on to reproduce were those whose beaks were most successful at getting food on their particular island. The finches without such beaks died off. Darwin drew pictures of the various finches, a simple example of survival of the fittest.

According to Darwin, through small gradual changes over millions of years, all the life forms on earth developed. When there were changes in the environment, species that did not develop the proper survival techniques died out, and new species developed to take their place. Darwin knew that often the offspring of parents sometimes developed traits that differed from their parents. These traits usually were negative, a kind of birth defect on the pathway of life. But sometimes these traits were positive, increasing the ability to survive and reproduce. But he did not understand how the process worked. The answer ultimately came from the work of the Austrian monk Gregor Mendel (1822–1884) and his work breeding pea plants. Mendel was the founder of genetics, the science as to how certain traits were passed down from generation to generation. The basic unit of such inheritance was called the gene.

Today we know that genes are made up of a double strand of a long nucleotide called DNA (deoxyribonucleic acid). The DNA gives a map for the creation of proteins, which are the basis of all metabolism. We have mapped the entire human genome, knowing the layout of all the genes that make up human beings. We know these genes are made up of long chains of nucleotides, joined in a double helix. We know how genes divide during reproduction. And we know that there are sometimes mutations, changes in one of those genes. Those mutations are the cause of the changes, both negative and positive, in offspring that are at the heart of natural selection. We use the term Neo-Darwinism, sometimes called the Modern Synthesis, for the combination of Darwin and Mendel, the process of how natural selection works. As we mentioned in the chapter on evil, brokenness or mutations are necessary for the development of life.

Neo-Darwinism is the accepted theory by almost all biologist on how life works. Scientists point to a great deal of evidence. For example, whales have flippers, birds have wings, mammals have front legs, and humans have arms. They fulfill very different functions in these different species. Yet they share the same bone structure. They seem to have evolved from a common ancestor. Fossils have been found that provide links between various species. All of this points to common ancestors. And genetics have shown that there is a gene pool shared by species across the board.

The process of evolution through natural selection explains how growth occurred organically, as we explained with the example of wisdom teeth. It makes scientific sense and explains multiple facts about life on earth. The question is whether this a totally material process, occurring by random chance. Given enough mutations and enough time, will the variety of species that we know have occurred? Is this really the blind watchmaker that Dawkins describes? This is the materialist view; it is a totally natural procedure that assumes no teleology, no final causes.

Many of us, myself included, are skeptical that this entire process could have begun totally by random chance. Let me share one example. What would have kicked off this entire process? We mentioned that DNA creates proteins. But it takes proteins to create DNA. What came first? It is an ancient chicken and egg question. I am moved by one passage in the Talmud, that speaks of ten miraculous items God manufactured at the dawn of creation. (We mentioned this earlier in the chapter on miracles.) One of those was "the tongs that held the tongs."[5] To make a pair of tongs, one must hold molten metal over the fire and shape it. A pair of tongs was used to hold this. But this pair had to be held by an earlier pair of tongs. Where did the first pair of tongs come from? Something had to start the process. The miracle is something kicked off the process. And I believe something besides random chance had to start the process we call life.

Microbiologist Leslie Orgel expresses this skepticism about the origin of life in an article in *Scientific American*:

> It is extremely improbable that proteins and nucleic acids, both of which are structurally complex, arose spontaneously in the same place at the same time. Yet it also seems impossible to have one without the other. And so, at first glance, one might have to

5. *Avot* 5:6.

conclude that life could never, in fact, have originated by chemical means.[6]

Orgel does explore the possibility of panspermia, the idea that life arose on another planet and was placed on Earth by an advanced civilization. But this idea does not solve the origin of life question, but it simply pushes it off to some other planet.

I agree with the scientific consensus that evolution by natural selection is the best explanation for life on earth. Where I disagree is with those like Dawkins who insist it is a blind process. I believe that somewhere along the way we need the idea of mind. Some theologians speak of theistic evolution, where God is involved in the details of mutations and natural selection, deciding which genes to mutate. However, in this chapter on materialism we have already mentioned that the universe is a closed system, and there are problems with a God who interferes from outside the system. It would add energy to the closed system.

When we spoke about entropy, we mentioned the idea that perhaps there is a low level of mental activity in the particles that make up the universe. This causes them to move from chaos to order. Perhaps such low-level mental activity can be used to explain evolution. This radical idea has found some acceptance among some biologists.

Epigenetics and Panpsychism

Nobel Laureate biologist George Wald published an article in the academic journal *Organic Chemistry* titled, "Life and Mind in the Universe." In his abstract at the beginning of the article, he writes:

> How is it that, with so many other apparent options, we are in a Universe that possesses just that particular nexus of properties that breeds life? It has occurred to me lately—I must confess with a certain shock to my scientific sensitivities . . . [that] mind, rather than emerging as a late outgrowth in the evolution of life, has existed always, as the matrix, the source and condition of physical reality—that the stuff of which physical reality is composed is mind-stuff. It is mind that has composed a physical universe, and that know and create: science-, art-, and technology-making animals.[7]

6. Orgel, "Origin," 78.
7. Wald, "Life and Mind," 160–61.

What is the role of mind in the process of evolution by natural selection that we have described? Materialists such as Dawkins would deny the presence of mind, saying that everything is matter in motion. Some materialists would admit that mind is an emergent property, that can only manifest itself when there is a certain degree of complexity. Some philosophers call a mind that emerges late in creation and then affects lower levels "top down causation." For me, it is difficult to see how such an emergent mind could not have an effect on the lower-level organic compounds that make up an organism. We will explore the issue of mind for materialists in the next chapter.

Evolutionary theists would say that God intervenes on the microscopic level, creating the mutations and other changes to move the evolutionary process forward. We have already stated that such divine intervention violates the laws of the conservation of energy, let alone the laws of entropy. This leaves one other possibility, which was the point of Wald's article. Perhaps there is a low-level consciousness that pervades everything in the universe. Perhaps, as philosopher David Chalmers has taught, there is mind all the way down. The name of this view is panpsychism. Perhaps the whole history of life on earth is driven by the behavior of genes, who have some inner sense of the direction they need to go in. If this is true, then evolution is not blind.

Other scientists are beginning to recognize this as a possibility. Biologist William Harmon together with Elisabet Sahtouris wrote a book titled *Biology Revisioned*. They quoted Wald's work:

> The major puzzles in the evolutionary picture, to this mind, could only be satisfactorily resolved by assuming that creative mind is not an emergent quality appearing only in the latter stages of the evolutionary process; creative mind appears to have been present all along, even before the first life forms. If we follow through with this kind of logic and ontological assumption, the story of evolution has a very different meaning from the accepted version.[8]

Harmon and Sahtouris claim in their book:

> As for consciousness, this mystery appears to be in some way at the heart of all the others. And intentionality, the appearance of purpose, is perhaps best thought of as part of the same puzzle. It is becoming increasingly apparent that an adequate dealing with the issue of consciousness is not just something scientists will

8. Harmon and Sahtouris, *Biology Revisioned*, pp. 160–161.

get around to in time; it is a basic challenge to the completeness of Western science that must be dealt with.[9]

The book continues with a radical statement, "*Mutations* of DNA is not only random; in some circumstances it appears to be purposeful."[10]

To explore this issue further, let me turn to a relatively new area of scientific study regarding genetics, epigenetics. To introduce this idea, let us turn first to a portion of the Torah and a selection from the Talmud. There is a story in the Torah that has confused me for years. The book of Genesis speaks about Jacob's cleverness when it comes to animal husbandry. Jacob has been working for his father-in-law, Laban, who is extremely crooked when it comes to money. Laban promises Jacob he can get all the newborn speckled and spotted goats and sheep as his salary. Then Laban secretly hides all such goats and sheep, so that only all white ones are left. Anyone who knows something about genetics knows that when solid white goats and sheep mate, they will probably have solid white baby goats and sheep. Laban is trying to cheat Jacob.

Jacob comes up with a clever trick. He takes poplar branches and makes rods, then has the goats and sheep mate while looking at the rods. Somehow what the goats see while they are mating affects the genetic make-up of their offspring, and they are born speckled and spotted. Jacob knows a secret, that genes react to what the goats and sheep see. Later this same idea will appear in rabbinic literature. Rabbi Yochanan was considered unusually handsome, the George Clooney of his day. The Talmud teaches that he would sit outside the mikvah in the evening so that women would look at him, conceive that night, and have handsome or beautiful babies.[11] Again, what someone sees before conceiving a newborn will affect the newborn.

To anyone who has studied modern biology, this sounds crazy. Genetics is a chemical process. Francis Crick, part of the team of Watson and Crick who discovered the double helix, describes what he calls the central dogma of biology. DNA affects RNA, which affects proteins. But proteins can never affect RNA to affect DNA. It is a one-way street, from inside out. It never goes from the outside in. What someone sees on the outside cannot affect their genome. We are the products of our genetics, pure chemicals, which are not affected by outside influences. How can something in the environment affect our genes? Jacob and the poplar branches, Rabbi Yochanan sitting at the mikvah, are silly stories from our past with no biological reality. Or are they?

9. Harmon and Sahtouris, *Biology Revisioned*, 7.

10. Harmon and Sahtouris, *Biology Revisioned*, 44.

11. *Babylonian Talmud Baba Metzia* 84a.

Today there is a whole new area of biology called epigenetics. It teaches that things in the environment can have a direct effect on how the human
genome works. Environmental influences including thoughts can turn on
or turn off certain genes, changing the results. Scientists give numerous
examples. Let me mention one. Scientists have studied the effects of babies
conceived and born in the Netherlands during the Dutch Hunger Winter of
1944–1945. Many babies born during this period were much slighter and
smaller boned. (A quick thought on this: My daughter has a picture of the
actress Audrey Hepburn in her living room. She was about eight years old
when Hepburn died, and I am sure she never saw the movie *Breakfast at
Tiffany's*. But something drew her to this beautiful if fragile-looking actress.
Audrey Hepburn was a teen in Holland during this period; perhaps the famine was responsible for her delicate look that was so appealing.) Scientists
have discovered that when many of these babies grew up and had children
of their own, the new generation was also affected. The famine that winter
influenced genetics for multiple generations. Environmental factors literally
changed the genes.

We live in an age that teaches a mechanistic view of everything. We
will come across Crick once again in the next chapter, where he shows that
he is an avid materialist. Everything has a material explanation. "My genes
made me do it." If Shakespeare had lived today, he would have had Cassius
say, "The fault dear Brutus is not in ourselves, but in our *genes*." We sense
that our genes control everything. But now we are saying something radically new. What happens in our environment can affect our genes. I am not
saying that if goats breed in front of poplar branches, they will come out
speckled and spotted. I am saying that if goats breed in a certain environment, perhaps in a place without tension or suffering, there is a good likeli-
hood the babies will come out stronger and healthier.

I am not a biologist, but I do sense that the central dogma of biology is
partially wrong. How can the environment affect our genes? Let me hint at
an idea suggested by a few scientists and philosophers willing to entertain a
radical idea. Perhaps our genes have a low level of consciousness that makes
them aware of their environment. Perhaps we can speak of consciousness
not as a higher-level phenomenon but something present in all material
things including organic chemicals. As mentioned above, the name for this
idea is panpsychism. It sounds crazy, but in the history of science, sometimes crazy ideas turn out to be true.

In the introduction to this book we looked at the work of the historian
of science Thomas Kuhn. Kuhn pointed out that science always works within a paradigm, seeking answers by doing research within that paradigm. Today, the paradigm for most biologists is a mechanistic view of the world and

Crick's central dogma. But according to Kuhn, when anomalies arise, there often arises a change in paradigm. This happened when Einstein's theory of gravitation replaced Newton's theory. Perhaps it will happen with further research in epigenetics, and the fact that events in the environment can affect genes. Already today some scientists are saying that Lamarck, long discredited, may have gotten something right. Perhaps the environment can affect genes. And perhaps the way it affects genes is the genes have some low level of perception of their environment, and have some sense of where they want evolution to lead. Perhaps Stephen Jay Gould is mistaken; if evolution could start all over, it would once again lead toward human beings. That is the direction that the genes want to go.

That brings us to one more important issue. What exactly does it mean to be a human in a world where life evolved from the primitive to the complex?

The Evolution of Humans

The publication of Darwin's *On the Origin of Species* (1859) was troubling to religious believers. Nonetheless, it is possible to accept evolution and still believe that humans are a special creation different in kind from the rest of the animal world. Far more troubling was Darwin's next book *The Descent of Man* (1871), which placed humans directly in the lineage of animals. Many religious people were deeply offended by the notion that there is no essential difference between humans and the rest of the animal kingdom.

Are humans just animals a little further along on the evolutionary chain? Personally, I find this belief troubling for two reasons. If humans are qualitatively the same as animals, we can raise up animals to be like humans, or we can lower humans to be like animals. Some will raise up animals to be like humans. If there is no difference between humans and animals, then if we speak of human rights we must in principle speak of animal rights. To do anything differently is to be guilty of what philosopher Peter Singer (b. 1946) calls speciesism.

Singer lays out his ideas in his book *Animal Liberation*.[12] Favoring humans over animals when it comes to rights or privileges is no different than favoring whites over blacks (racism), men over women (sexism), or straights over gays (homophobia). To follow through on Singer's insight, not only would it be wrong to eat animals or use their products for clothing or cosmetics, but zoos, circuses, and even pets would be forbidden. There have been attempts to pass such animal rights legislation in various states and

12. Singer, *Animal Liberation*.

there have been court cases about speciesism, so far without success. But according to this point of view, it would be morally wrong to attribute any superior status to humans.

This approach concerns me, but I am far more concerned about the opposite point of view. If humans are merely animals, then there is nothing wrong with treating humans as we treat animals. Humans are no more given any special dignity than animals in a feed lot. In fact, People for the Ethical Treatment of Animals (PETA) said this by comparing the killing of six million Jews to the killing of six billion chickens. It was a holocaust of chickens. Such language cheapens the word "holocaust." In fact, the Nazi regime began their war against the Jewish people by treating them as animals, often using the term "vermin."

I can accept evolution and even the descent of man as Darwin put it. But at some point in that process there was a qualitative change, a creature with a new ontological status. To study this idea further, let us turn to the second creation story in the Bible, one that we have not yet considered in this book. It is the story of Adam and Eve in the Garden of Eden. God creates a beautiful garden as a paradise for Adam and his wife, Eve. The name Adam is not a particular name, but a generic name for man, or perhaps mankind. Eve, in Hebrew *Chava*, simply means "life," again a generic name for women who are the mothers of all life. Adam and Eve live in paradise, naked but not ashamed, their food being provided. They are told that they can eat everything in the garden except the fruit of the Tree of Knowledge of Good and Evil.

Most of us know the story. The snake tempts Eve and she eats of the fruit. (Nowhere does it say that the fruit is an apple.) Eve then gives the fruit to her husband and he eats. Adam and Eve are ashamed and hide from God. God asks them whether they ate from the forbidden fruit. God punishes the snake, making him crawl on his belly. God then punishes the woman, saying that in pain will she bring forth children. God punishes the man, saying that by the sweat of his brow will he bring forth bread to eat. Finally, God exiles Adam and Eve from the garden into the real world as we know it.

What does the story mean? We all have heard the classical understanding in Western culture that this is the story of the fall of mankind. The snake is really Satan in disguise. Tempted by Satan, Adam and Eve eat of the fruit and bring sin unto the world. As the popular saying goes, "By Adam's fall, sinners all." The great Catholic thinker Augustine of Hippo (354–430) saw this as a story of original sin, and how the perfect world God made became corrupted by humanity's act. John Milton wrote his classic epic poem *Paradise Lost*, describing Satan's rebellion against God and the desire to bring down the world God had made. In fact, many see this story as an explanation for evil in the world.

Nonetheless, this Western view of the story as the fall of humanity is not the only explanation of this parable. Allow me to suggest an alternative interpretation. I have always seen the Garden of Eden story not as a fall but as a rise. Humanity rose from being animal like to a new level of existence. It is the story of humanity rising above the animal, reaching a higher level of being.

Let us explore this. In the Garden of Eden we were naked and not ashamed. Who lives naked and not ashamed but animals (and young children who have not yet learned right from wrong)? In Eden our food was taken care of. We did not need to plant wheat in order to eat bread. It is the story of us being mere animals. Of course, place something tempting in front of an animal, they will eat it. Putting a beautiful piece of fruit in front of humanity and saying "don't eat" is like putting a dog biscuit in front of your pet and saying "don't eat." God knew that humanity would eat. According to Jewish tradition, the snake is not Satan but simply the human appetite, what Jews call the *yetzer hara*.

Humanity ate from the tree and reached a new level of being. For the first time, humanity could differentiate between good and evil. They could make moral choices. Adam and Eve were embarrassed at being naked and covered themselves with fig leaves. But God covered them with animal skins, symbolic that they were no longer animals but something qualitatively different.

The story is about the evolution of man from mere animals to something more than animals. It is closer to Darwin than Milton. It is about the rise of human beings into creatures who could make moral choices, who could speak, who could worship God, and who would eventually become God's partners in perfecting this world. It is the beginning of raising the world to a higher level. That is why I speak not of the fall of man but of the rise of man.

I believe that evolution by natural selection gives the best account of the diversity of living organisms across the earth. But I believe that it was not a blind process; behind it there was a mind or an image of the direction such evolution is going. David Ray Griffin, a modern interpreter of Whitehead's process philosophy, makes this point precisely:

> One of the reasons for the rejection of theistic evolutionism has been the absence of any idea how a divine actuality could influence the evolutionary process. Much of the problem has been due to materialism, which portrays nature as composed

of vacuous bits of matter which can be causally affected only by other bits of matter. Process philosophy overcomes this problem with panexperientialism [his word for panpsychism], according to which nature is composed of prehensive occasions of experience. The doctrine, by explaining how cells, molecules, and even electrons in the human body can be influenced by the human mind, thereby explain how all the components of the world can be influenced by a Cosmic Mind.[13]

Griffin's book suggested the direction of my own thinking. I wrote my PhD dissertation on process philosophy and the Jewish mystical view of the creation story. I will share more details of my thinking in Part III of this book. For now, all I can say is that evolution is not a blind process, but it leads in a direction. The direction is humanity.

I truly believe that one can be deeply religious and still see evolution as the best explanation for the variety of life on earth. Let me quote the Orthodox former chief rabbi of Palestine, Rabbi Abraham Isaac Kook. It is an unusually pro-evolution point of view for a very Orthodox rabbi:

> The theory of evolution is increasingly conquering the world at this time, and, more so than all other philosophical theories, conforms to the kabbalistic secrets of the world. Evolution, which proceeds on a path of ascendancy, provides an optimistic foundation for the world. How is it possible to despair at a time when we see that everything evolves and ascends? When we penetrate the inner meaning of the ascending evolution, we find in it the divine element shining with absolute brilliance. It is precisely the *Ein Sof* in actuality which manages to bring to realization that which is *Ein Sof* in potential.[14]

In a similar way, let us turn to a Christian paleontologist and Jesuit Priest Pierre Teilhard de Chardin (1881–1955), who built an entire theology based on evolution. He envisioned a world moving from the mineral to the animal to the human to what he called the Omega Point, a place of shared minds. He envisioned this long before the internet was invented. He taught that the desire to unite with others begins at the lowest level of being. "If there were no real internal propensity to unite, even at a prodigiously rudimentary level—indeed in the molecule itself—it would be physically impossible for love to appear higher up."[15] This seems to fit the panpsychism we spoke about earlier in this chapter. On every level, from the molecule to

13. Griffin, *Reenchantment*, 213.

14. Kook, *Orot HaKodesh* II:537.

15. Teilhard de Chardin, *Phenomenon*, 264.

the human person, beings must give up their individuality to move toward a shared whole: "The peak of ourselves, the acme of our originality, is not our individuality but our person; and according to the evolutionary structure of our world, we can only find our person by uniting together."[16] In another essay, de Chardin famously taught, "Everything that rises must converge."[17] Flannery O'Conner (1925–1964) used his quote as the title of her famous story about a mother and a son in the old South, coping with the new civil rights movement.

Finally, let us end this chapter on evolution with a quote from the great Sufi mystic poet Jalal ad-Din Muhammad Rumi (1207–1273). Although Rumi lived more than half a millennium before Darwin, his vision of the evolution of the soul has an almost Darwinian feel to it:

> I died as mineral and became a plant,
> I died as plant and rose to animal,
> I died as animal and I was man.
> Why should I fear? When was I less by dying?
> Yet once more I shall die as man, to soar
> With angels blest; but even from angelhood
>
> I must pass on: all except God doth perish.
> When I have sacrificed my angel soul,
> I shall become what no mind e'er conceived.
> Oh, let me not exist! for non-existence
>
> Proclaims in organ tones, 'To Him we shall return.'

---

16. Teilhard de Chardin, *Phenomenon*, 263.
17. Teilhard de Chardin, *Building the Earth*, 11.

CHAPTER 7

Mind—Could a Robot Have a Soul?

The pragmatic philosopher William James tells the story of a new philosopher professor who comes to a college campus. There are two philosophy clubs, the House of Determinism and the House of Free Will. The new professor debates which club to join. First, he goes to the House of Determinism. They ask him, "why do you want to join here?" He says, "I made a choice." "In that case, you do not belong here," they say, so they throw him out. Then he goes to the House of Free Will. They ask him, "why do you want to join here?" He says, "I had no choice." "In that case," they say, "you do not belong here," so they threw him out.

I attended a workshop on making our synagogue a more welcoming place. The facilitator asked, what do visitors see when they enter your building? What happens when they go on your webpage? What happens when they walk into the building and try to find the office? The sanctuary? The restrooms? And what happens when they call your synagogue on the phone? Then he looked at us and said, "If someone calls the main synagogue number and gets a machine instead of a human being, then your synagogue is not a welcoming place." That hit home. We have such an electronic answering machine.

Our answering machine contains a menu of options, like most businesses. You have to push the right number to reach a human being. I was tempted to say to the facilitator, what if it is a really sophisticated answering machine? What if it is machine so good that the caller does not know if he or she is talking to a machine or a person? It dawned on me that this was the same question that Alan Turing, one of the inventors of the computer, had asked at the dawn of the information age.

What Is a Mind?

I often use the terms "soul" and "mind" interchangeably. They both refer to the subjective, the conscious, that which is not matter, the cognitive and perceptive part of our being. Both soul and mind are the "I" in each of us. Nonetheless, to philosophers there is a difference. The soul is a separate entity from the body, something that might survive the death of the body. For dualists like Plato and Descartes, the soul exists, and it will continue to exist after we die. Philosopher Gilbert Ryle cynically called it "the ghost in the machine." But to materialists there is no soul, no separate entity that survives a body. To materialists such as Hobbes, Marx, and Dawkins, we have no soul, something that survives after we die. But we do have a mind.

The mind is one of the functions of the body. It is what the brain does. Our stomachs digest, our hearts beat, our muscles move, and our brain "minds." As human beings, the mind is something we do. The mind may perish when the body perishes—it needs a brain to function. But while we are alive, even if we have no soul, we have a mind. We have something that thinks, that perceives, that decides, that creates a sense of self. For materialists, that interplay between the mind and the body is one of the most difficult problems in philosophy.

To many materialists, the mind is a mere epiphenomenon. It has no real existence. It is an outgrowth of the functioning of the body, but it can have no material influence on the body. It is like the picture on a television. It can be seen, but somebody in the television picture cannot reach out and turn off the television. That would be extremely strange. So too, if our material body reaches a certain level of complexity, something called "mind" emerges. It has no reality beyond an emergent property of the body, and it cannot reach back and affect the body. It is like the television picture, like a shadow, or like smoke that comes out of a jet engine, but the only thing that has reality is the material substructure. In some substantive sense, only the material exists.

This image raises numerous questions for materialists. Does this mind have free will? How come it seems we can influence material events? And how does subjectivity emerge, the sense of self that we all feel? The existence of a conscious mind is the most difficult problem faced by materialists.

Free Will and Determinism

One of the oldest and most difficult debates in the history of philosophy
is the question, do we have free will or is everything determined? We believe that we make free choices. The philosophical name for such free will
is libertarianism (not the political party, but the belief in free will.) But if
everything is material, and material events happen in accordance with the
laws of physics, are all our choices predetermined by those laws? Moreover,
if everything is predetermined, why should we punish criminals, who are
acting out by predetermined laws? Already this issue can be found in the
Bible. God hardens Pharaoh's heart, causing him to stubbornly refuse to let
the Israelites go. Then he punishes Pharaoh for this very stubbornness. Isn't
God being unfair?

 One of the answers I often give is that Pharaoh had free will; he hardened his own heart through the first six plagues. Only then does the Torah
say that God hardened Pharaoh's heart. When we do the wrong thing often
enough, it soon becomes a habit, part of our very nature. It is as if God
made us that way. The rabbis of the Talmud would say the same thing, saying that "the evil inclination is at first like a spider web, then like a heavy
rope of a cart."[1] At first it is easy to overcome the evil inclination and do the
right thing, but then the evil inclination literally ties us down. We have free
choice, but if we make the wrong choice often enough, we no longer have
such free will. Our bad behavior takes away our free will. Or as the midrash
puts it, "Resh Lakish responded . . . God gives a person one, two, and three
opportunities to do repentance. If he does not repent, God locks his heart
from repentance to punish him for his sin."[2]

 Of course, the Talmud, and Jewish tradition, assumes we have free
will. The Bible quotes God telling Cain before he kills his brother Abel,
"sin crouches at the door but you can rule over it" (Genesis 4:7). Tradition
assumes that we have a body and a soul, and that soul can freely choose.
Jewish tradition is dualist. What about materialists? To materialists there is
only the body. Could such a material entity have free will? It is an extremely
difficult issue for materialists, who usually reject libertarianism in favor of
some kind of determinism. In determinism, everything that happens has a
cause. All of our actions, all of our decisions, thus have a cause. Free will is
an illusion.

 One of the most famous examples of an argument against free will
was used by Clarence Darrow defending Nathan Leopold and Richard Loeb,

1. *Babylonian Talmud Sukkot* 52a.
2. *Sh'mot Rabbah* 13:3.

two young men accused of murdering a younger boy, Bobby Franks, for the thrill of it. They almost committed the perfect crime, but they were caught and put on trial. Darrow was hired to defend the boys and succeeded in getting them prison terms rather than the death penalty. Here is part of his argument at the 1924 trial:

> "Why did they kill little Bobby Franks? Not for money, not for spite; not for hate. They killed him as they might kill a spider or a fly, for the experience. They killed him because they were made that way. Because somewhere in the infinite processes that go to the making up of the boy or the man something slipped, and those unfortunate lads sit here hated, despised, outcasts, with the community shouting for their blood."[3]

Forces beyond their control drove these two young men to commit murder; they had no free will.

Scientists have also sought to demonstrate that free will is an illusion. In an often cited 1983 experiment in neuroscience, Benjamin Libet (1916–2007) challenged the idea that conscious decisions affect neural actions. He found that neural actions begin within the body 350 milliseconds before the subject made the conscious decision to take such actions. The body has already decided before the mind is even aware of taking action. Volumes have been written about this experiment, mostly by materialists who see it as proof that free will is an illusion.

Some philosophers have attempted to rescue the idea of free will by differentiating between what they call hard determinism and soft determinism. Hard determinism says that everything has been decided; there is no choice. Soft determinism, often called compatibilism, says that both free will and determinism are possible. If I have free will, then I have a choice to follow my will. If I want to eat ice cream before I go to bed, it is totally my choice. But where did my will come from? My desire to eat ice cream was determined long ago, established by forces beyond my control. Our will is determined, but we have the choice to follow that will.

Some modern thinkers tried to solve the problem of free will by turning to quantum mechanics. Quantum mechanics is a probabilistic theory of reality. For example, in a collection of atoms one such atom may have a fifty-fifty chance of decaying within an hour, but it is impossible to predict whether any particular atom will decay. Atomic decay is random and undetermined. That is why Einstein hated quantum mechanics, saying that "God does not play dice with the universe." If events are random, perhaps

---

3. Sommers, "Darrow and Determinism."

this is the basis of free will. (We will have much more to say about quantum mechanics later in the chapter on light.)

The problem with using quantum mechanics to speak of free will is that the randomness only works for individual atoms. Put billions of atoms together and the number that will decay is not random, but predetermined. In our case, an atom perhaps will decay in an hour and perhaps not; if there are billions of atoms, then half will decay within that hour. We say this atom has a half-life of one hour. There may be indeterminacy for each individual atom but not for the group. As a group, everything is predetermined. Quantum mechanics deals with randomness and uncertainty at a micro-level. But we live our lives at a macro-level, where randomness does not exist. Quantum mechanics is not an answer to the question of free will.

Determinism, whether hard or soft, is the prevalent viewpoint today among philosophers and scientists. In fact, some social scientists are seriously rethinking our entire penal system. Why should we punish criminals if they have no choice over their actions, but are driven, like Leopold and Loeb, by some inner drives? What does it mean to live in a world without free will, where everything is predetermined?

Having said that, there are materialists who are strong advocates of free will. Existentialism teaches that we are free to choose the kind of people we wish to be. As Jean-Paul Sartre (1905–1980) famously defined existentialism, "existence comes before essence." We exist in the world. In fact, the famous existentialist Martin Heidegger (1889–1976) taught that we are literally thrust into the world. We have no essence, no purpose, or to use Aristotle famous phrase, no final cause. We simply exist. But we do have absolute freedom to create ourselves into the kind of people we wish to be. Sadly, for the history of philosophy, Heidegger created himself into a Nazi.

The roots of existential thinking began with such nineteenth-century thinkers as Soren Kierkegaard (1813–1855) and Friedrich Nietzsche (1844–1900). Both taught that we exist in the world without any essence, any established purpose. We have the absolute freedom to create ourselves. For Kierkegaard, who was a Christian, this meant taking a leap of faith toward God, even if such belief in God is absurd. Kierkegaard's hero was the biblical Abraham, who had faith in God to the point of sacrificing his own son. Nietzsche, on the other hand, taught that "God is dead" and Western religion is broken. We have the freedom to create ourselves and become God, making ourselves into what Nietzsche called an ubermensch or superman. We will have more to say about Nietzsche in our chapter on nature. It is noteworthy that both Kierkegaard and Nietzsche built their philosophies on absolute freedom.

When I went to college everyone was becoming an existentialist. They were quoting Sartre, his regular lover Simone de Beauvoir (1908–1986), and novelist Albert Camus (1913–1960). Life was absurd and meaningless. Existentialism fit perfectly the materialistic mood of those times that the world is here by random forces with no God and no creator. In such a world, we have the freedom to create ourselves. Camus, in one of most famous essays, compared this world to the ancient Greek god Sisyphus, forced to roll a rock up a hill just to have it roll down again. In this absurd situation Sisyphus had to find meaning. Such absolute freedom is frightening. That is why Sartre famously taught, "Man is condemned to be free."

So who is correct? Are the determinists correct, who say that our freedom is an illusion, that the inner workings of nerve synapses in our brain control our actions? Are the compatibilists correct, who say that we can follow our will, but what we will has been predetermined? Are the libertarians correct who say, never mind the laws of physics, we have free will? Or are the existentialists correct when they say that we are condemned to be free?

Philosophers will argue about this forever. But deep in my heart, I cannot accept total determinism. I believe we have a mind, and that mind has free will. But what does it mean to have a mind in a material world? That is the next question we will explore.

Material Views of Mind

In 1974 Thomas Nagel published a classic essay on philosophy of mind called, "What Is It Like to Be a Bat?"[4] The goal of the essay was not to study the bat as an outsider, as a scientist may look at the behavior of bats. Nor was it to imagine what a human would feel pretending to be a bat, imagining using sonar to find one's way. Rather, it was to claim that there is a subjective experience that a bat would have, which no human being could ever imagine. Nagel writes:

> I assume we all believe that bats have experience. After all, they are mammals, and there is no more doubt that they have experience than that mice or pigeons or whales have experience. I have chosen bats instead of wasps or flounders because if one travels too far down the phylogenetic tree people gradually shed their faith that there is experience there at all. Bats, although more closely related to us than those other species, nevertheless

4. T. Nagel, "What Is It Like."

present a range of activity and a sensory apparatus so different
from ours that the problem I want to pose is exceptionally vivid.[5]

Nagel is attempting to show that there is a limit to physicalism, what
we can know through scientific inquiry. Science tries to present reality as
subject to objective study, trying to give us a God's eye view, or what Nagel
called in his 1986 book, *The View from Nowhere*. But science is limited. According to Nagel, the best objective science can never get into the head of a
bat, or any other species. To have consciousness means "there is something
like being something." There is an inside subjective view that science cannot not touch. Even human consciousness seems to be beyond the ability
of science. Mind is a reality beyond physicalism. Nagel seems to be falling
back on the kind of dualism we discussed in the previous section. But any
attempt to understand how mind emerges from a material world stumbles
on the question, how does subjectivity emerge from the material?

Let us look briefly at three answers on the problem of mind often
presented by scientists and philosophers. Each of these is subject to a great
deal of discussion among thinkers, and here we can only scratch the surface.
Nonetheless, each tries to answer the question of the meaning of mind in a
physical world.

The first answer often given is behaviorism. We cannot know the inner workings of a mind or peer inside the head of another person, or any
other living creature. All we can see is how they behave in various situations. Behaviorism teaches that we cannot even talk about subjective mental
experiences. We can only talk about behaviors, how someone or something
acts in various situations. Mind is simply behavior. This became the basis
of B. F. Skinner's (1904–1990) theory of psychology—treat the behavior,
not the inner being. This fits in with the logical positivist's theory that all
we can know is what we can verify empirically. Logical positivism was the
most popular philosophical approach in the early twentieth century. It grew
among a group of thinkers known as the Vienna Circle. The central idea
was we can only know what we can verify. We cannot verify the existence of
minds, but we can verify behavior.

This idea may be very useful in the psychological treatment of patients.
But it seems to deny one of the fundamental facts about the universe. We
all know that we have a mind. Descartes put this at the core of his system of
thought. Descartes was searching for something indubitable, without doubt.
He concluded that he could not doubt his own mind. *Cogito Ergo Sum*—"I
think therefore I am."

---

5. T. Nagel, "What Is It Like," 438.

David Chalmers, who we have already discussed regarding the hard problem of consciousness, raises the question of philosophical zombies. These are not the zombies we see in the movies, not the brain-eating creatures of *Night of the Living Dead*. To philosophers like Chalmers, a zombie is a person who acts like a human in every way, including their behavior. However, a zombie has no consciousness. It is a being who we think of as human by their activities, but there is no inner self. There is a brain but no mind. The idea of philosophical zombies becomes an important thought experiment created by many philosophers of mind to pin down what we mean by consciousness.

Such zombies behave in every way like humans, without having any consciousness. We would be hard pressed to tell if someone were a zombie or an actual person with a mind. (This issue will come up later when we speak about the Turing test.) Chalmers claims that since we can conceive of such a creature, even if none exist in reality, then mind must be something more than behavior. Mind must be a separate entity. As mentioned earlier, Chalmers in his philosophy of mind is a kind of dualist, who see mind as something fundamental to the universe and separate from matter. Materialist philosopher Daniel Dennett (b. 1942), in his book *Consciousness Explained*,[6] claims that such philosophical zombies could not exist in reality and therefore we cannot learn anything from them.

A second answer very popular among materialists is what they call mind–brain identity theory. We can speak about a mind and we can speak about a brain, but they are both referring to the same thing. It is as if we use the words "morning star" and "evening star" like two separate entities, and then realize that both phrases refer to the planet Venus. We have used different terms for mind and brain because our knowledge was limited. As our knowledge increases about neuroscience, we know that mind and brain are really the same thing. In fact, today scientists can map out the physical brain to show how various parts cause various mental events.

One of the strongest advocates of this point of view is Francis Crick, co-discoverer of the double helix of DNA. Crick has written in his book *The Astonishing Hypothesis*, "You, your joys and sorrows, your memories and ambitions, your sense of identity and free will, are in fact no more than the behavior of a vast assembly of nerve cells and their associated molecules."[7] If we could study the human brain to the last detail, we would know everything there is to know about the human mind.

---

6. Dennett, *Consciousness.*

7. Crick, *Astonishing Hypothesis*, 3.

This idea is troubling to many individuals including scientists. The Canadian brain surgeon Wilder Penfield (1891–1976), whose patients were often kept conscious when he performed surgery, was able to get patients to identify various brain functions such as viewing color or hearing sounds, and what part of the brain causes them. But when he asked patients to tell him where the "I" was, the basic seat of subjectivity, it could not be pinned down to any one place. There was something beyond the physical brain causing perception and movement. Often dualists claim that Penfield proved the existence of the soul. Perhaps they are overreaching, but his findings seem to indicate that the mind is not simply the brain.

One of the most quoted thought experiments to challenge mind–brain identity theory came from the Australian philosopher Frank Jackson (b. 1943). He imagined a scientist named Mary who had been raised from birth in a black-and-white world. He pictured Mary raised from the beginning in a room where everything was deliberately kept black and white including her own skin. Perhaps a better possibility is that she was color blind, unable to see any colors at all. Nonetheless, Mary was the foremost expert on the physical properties of the color red. She knew exactly what wave lengths caused objects to be red, what part of the eye responded to that red, and how the brain processed red. One day she had surgery that allowed her for the first time to see red. Suddenly she had something new, the subjective experience of red. Jackson pointed out that seeing red is something more than mere physicalism, something subjective. Philosophers call these subjective experiences qualia. How can we explain through pure physics the qualia of seeing red, tasting coffee, feeling pain, or for that matter, falling in love? (In fairness to Jackson, he later rejected his own argument. I still find the argument compelling.)

There is a third approach to a material view of the mind, probably the most popular today, which we quoted at the beginning of this chapter. Mind is not a thing. Rather it is a function. Mind is how the brain functions, like digestion is how the stomach functions. Various material structures—a human brain, a robot, a computer—can all instantiate this function called mind. Materialists defend functionalism as the best explanation of what we call consciousness.

In his 1904 essay "Does Consciousness Exist," the pragmatic philosopher William James, who invented the phrase "stream of consciousness," asserts that consciousness is not a thing but a function. It is not a noun but a verb. James writes:

> Let me then immediately explain that I mean only to deny that
> the word [consciousness] stands for an entity, but to insist most

emphatically that it does stand for a function. There is, I mean, no aboriginal stuff or quality of being, contrasted with that of which material objects are made, out of which our thoughts of them are made; but there is a function in experience which thoughts perform, and for the performance of which this quality of being is invoked.[8]

By asserting that consciousness is not a separate substance, we escape the dualism of Descartes. There is a substance called matter that sometimes functions in a particular way, which we will call mind.

My favorite challenge to the functional theory of mind comes from the philosopher John Searle (b. 1932) in his famous Chinese room thought experiment. Searle imagines a man in a room being fed Chinese characters through the door. He has a book of instructions how to react to all the various characters he is fed. If he receives various characters, he passes out through the door other Chinese characters. The man is following instructions. To an outsider, it looks like the person in the room is speaking Chinese. The problem is that the man does not know a word of Chinese. He is able through rules to deal with the syntax of Chinese. But he has no idea of the semantics of Chinese.

Functionalism is often used by advocates of artificial intelligence that computers have minds that function like human minds. Those who challenge such artificial intelligence say that like the man in the Chinese room, the computer is merely manipulating symbols. Computers understand syntax but have no sense of semantics. Searle's thought experiment seems to point to the fact that an understanding mind is more than a material object, leading back to a kind of dualism. Of course, many philosophers have raised objections to Searle's as well as to Jackson's thought experiments. And so the argument about mind and matter continues.

Functionalism and computers raises the question of the famous Turing test, raised by one of the greatest minds of the twentieth century, Alan Turing (1912–1954). Born in Britain, Turing helped Great Britain win World War II by breaking the Nazi war code Enigma. The 2014 movie *The Imitation Game* tells the story of Turing and his team breaking the code. Turing also conceived a theoretical machine with an infinitely long tape, with various characters on the tape, and rules that would apply for whatever letter shows up. This became that theoretical basis for the modern computer, which is simply a non-infinite Turing machine. Sadly, Turing committed suicide after being arrested for the crime of homosexuality.

8. James, "Does Consciousness Exist?" 478.

Turing conceived a famous test of the intelligence of machines. Imagine a person feeding questions to either a human being or a machine behind a closed door. The person has no knowledge whether a human being or a machine is answering the questions. If after a certain amount of time the person feeding the questions cannot tell if a person or a machine is responding, then for all intents and purpose the machine is a person. A machine that passes the Turing test can be considered a person with consciousness. Today, regular contests are held to see if someone can develop a machine that would pass the Turing test. There is an annual contest for the Loebner Prize, given to the machine that comes closest to passing the Turing test. So far no computer programmer has won the grand prize.

My own sense is that no matter how fancy a machine, it would not have the subjective ability to perceive qualia that we would call consciousness. One of the fascinating questions of science fiction is whether we can build a robot or a computer with a human soul. Science fiction from *2001: Space Odyssey* to *I, Robot* to *Westworld* deal with this question. The Greeks dealt with it in the legend of Pygmalion, the sculptor who carves a woman and then fell in love with her. This is the basis of the George Bernard Shaw play *Pygmalion* and the Broadway classic *My Fair Lady*. Of course, Mary Shelley raised the same theme in her classic novel *Frankenstein*.

Jewish tradition has dealt with the same question. The Talmud teaches, "Rava created a person, and sent it before Rav Zeira. Rav Zeira spoke to it, but it wouldn't reply Rav Zeira said to it you are a creation of one of my colleagues, return to your dust. Rav Hanina and Rav Ushaya would sit all of Erev Shabbat, occupied with a Book of Creation, and create for themselves a third-grown calf, and they would eat it."[9] This story about Rava became the basis of one of the great legends of Judaism, that of the Golem created by Rabbi Judah Lowe known as the Maharal of Prague (1520–1609). The rabbi created a man called a Golem from the dust and used God's name to bring it to life, so it could protect the Jewish people. When he felt he was losing control of his Golem he removed God's name and sent it back to dust. Today, Jews will use the phrase "Golem" for somewhat dull-witted, who lacks basic sense. But the legend is about an artificial man.

Is the Golem truly human? Could we count him in the minyan? Would we be forbidden to harm him, let alone kill him? Is it even possible to make an artificial person? I have my own feelings about this question. To answer, let me turn to the work of the one twentieth-century mathematician who matched Turing in brilliance, Kurt Gödel.

---

9. *Babylonian Talmud Sanhedrin* 65b.

Could Robots Have Souls?

Before I started my rabbinic studies, I was a mathematics major. I even began graduate work in theoretical mathematics. So when I was a newly ordained rabbi, a mathematician friend gave me book that he said I would enjoy. It was Douglas Hofstadter's *Gödel, Escher, Bach: An Eternal Golden Braid*.[10] I fell in love with the book, which reminded me of *Alice in Wonderland*. At the heart of the book was a logical theorem that revolutionized mathematics in the twentieth century.

In 1931, Austrian logician Kurt Gödel (1906–1978) shocked the world of mathematics with a theorem known as the incompleteness theorem. Until then mathematicians believed that if you have simple definitions and axioms, plus the rules of logic, you could prove everything that needed to be proven in mathematics. Take the axioms, use the rules to prove theorem after theorem, and like Euclid, all the possible theorems would follow. In fact, a computer could be programmed with the basic axioms and theorems, and churn out everything there is to know in mathematics.

Gödel began by assuming that this formal system of axioms and rules included the natural numbers: 1, 2, 3, and so on. He then established a sentence that was part of the system and which made the following claim: "this sentence is not provable in this mathematical system." The sentence is true. And the sentence is not provable. The details are not difficult and can be studied in the book *Gödel's Proof* by Ernest Nagel and James R. Neuman.[11] At the heart of the proof was the idea of self-reference, sentences that talk about themselves. The classic example is the sentence, "This sentence is false." If the sentence is false, then the sentence is true. But if the sentence is true, then the sentence is false. It is a paradox. Another example is the male barber who lives in a town, and shaves the beards of all the men and only the men who do not shave their own beards. Does the barber shave his own beard? If he does, then he does not. But if he does not, then he does. Again, we have a paradox.

Gödel stood mathematics on its head by proving that for any logical system including the numbers, there is a true statement. But this true statement cannot be proven within the logical system. There are statements that are true but unprovable. But a computer, which works by an algorithm, is a logical system that includes the natural numbers. Computers work by logical rules. Therefore, we can come up with a true statement that the computer cannot prove.

10. Hofstadter, *Gödel, Escher, Bach*.
11. Nagel and Neuman, *Gödel's Proof*.

How does this relate to whether or not robots have souls? Let us suppose that our mind is simply a computer, like a robot with a soul. We turn to the work of J. R. Lucas, who published an article in 1961 titled "Minds, Machines, and Gödel." This work was further developed by Roger Penrose in his 1989 book *The Emperor's New Mind*. The argument is therefore called the Lucas–Penrose argument.

According to Lucas–Penrose, let us suppose the human mind is a computer, working by a set algorithm on basic axioms, using the laws of logic. Then everything we know would be a theorem within that system, provable by the computer that is our mind. But we know that we can come up with a sentence that says, "this sentence is not provable by the computer that is our mind." From Gödel we know the sentence is true. But if our mind is a mere computer, we could not know that sentence. We come up with a contradiction, something we both know and do not know. Therefore, our mind is more than a computer. There are things we know by self-reference, looking at our own mind, that no computer could know.

I am aware that this is all a bit complicated, and worth looking at again. The Lucas–Penrose is subtle and takes careful thought. But it seems to lead to the conclusion that computers or robots could not have a soul. And if that is true, we humans are more than either computers or robots. Not everyone is convinced by the Lucas–Penrose argument, and there is an entire literature on whether it proves what they tried to prove. But I find it convincing. Deep in my heart, I do not believe that a computer can have a knowledge of its self. Nagel could write about what it is like to be a bat. But he could not write about what it is like to be a computer. A computer is a mere machine, like the man in the room pushing around Chinese characters. It lacks the self-knowledge and awareness that makes us human.

We have looked at dualism and we have looked at materialism. Both are problematic. It is time to turn to a third creation story; this one gives a far more mystical view of reality. The approach is called idealism, the belief that mind rather than matter is the fundamental reality.

PART III

The Third Creation Story—Idealism

א בְּרֵאשִׁית בָּרָא אֱלֹהִים אֵת הַשָּׁמַיִם וְאֵת הָאָרֶץ: ב וְהָאָרֶץ הָיְתָה תֹהוּ וָבֹהוּ
וְחֹשֶׁךְ עַל־פְּנֵי תְהוֹם וְרוּחַ אֱלֹהִים מְרַחֶפֶת עַל־פְּנֵי הַמָּיִם: ג וַיֹּאמֶר אֱלֹהִים יְהִי־אוֹר
ד וַיַּרְא אֱלֹהִים אֶת־הָאוֹר כִּי־טוֹב וַיַּבְדֵּל אֱלֹהִים בֵּין הָאוֹר וּבֵין הַחֹשֶׁךְ:
ה וַיִּקְרָא אֱלֹהִים | לָאוֹר יוֹם וְלַחֹשֶׁךְ קָרָא לָיְלָה וַיְהִי־עֶרֶב וַיְהִי־בֹקֶר יוֹם אֶחָד:

"With wisdom _____ created God, Who is the heaven and the earth.
And on the earth matter and form were separated; and darkness was upon the
face of the deep. And the Spirit of God moved upon the face of the waters. And
God said, Let light flow into the world: and there was light. And God saw the
light, that it was good: and God divided the light from the darkness. And God
called the light Day, and the darkness he called Night. And the evening and the
morning were the first day."

(GENESIS 1:1–5)

CHAPTER 8

Idealism—What If Only Mind Exists?

Two monks were arguing about a flag blowing in the wind. One monk said, "it is the flag that is waving." The second monk said, "no, it is the wind that is waving." Back and forth they went. Finally, they went to ask the great Zen teacher Hui Neng. He answered, "my fellow monks, you are both wrong. It is not the flag that moves and it is not the wind that moves. It is your mind that moves."

As a rabbi, I love to quote that great compendium of Jewish law and lore known as the Talmud. One quote I have both heard from others and used myself is the maxim, "We do not see the world as it is. We see the world as we are." It is lovely quote that reflects my own beliefs, but unfortunately this quote never appears in the Talmud. The quote comes from the French–Cuban novelist and essayist Anais Nin (1903–1977). It appears in her novel *Seduction of the Minotaur* (1961). In the novel, Nin claims that this line comes from the Talmud. The line in the Talmud is not quite as powerful: "A man is shown only what is suggested by his own thoughts."[1] The quote shows that even mainstream rabbinic Judaism, the source of modern Judaism, suggests ideas that are close to idealism.

---

1. *Babylonian Talmud Berakhot* 55b.

What Is Idealism?

We have now reached our third creation story, the story presented in the great book of Jewish mysticism *The Zohar*. Here we find a radical reworking of the creation story. Here it is not God the subject creating the universe, the object. The nouns are reversed. Here God is the object, something creates God. The subject, whoever is doing the creating, is unknown and unknowable, what mystics call both *Ein Sof*—"Without End" and *Ayin*—"Nothing." Out of that nothing comes a universe which is God. If *Ein Sof* emanated its very being into the universe, then everything is part of God.

In this section we will explore the idea that God is mind, that in the beginning there was a primordial mind. This mind was unknowable. However, through an act of will that mind flowed out into space and time to create a universe. But now the universe itself is mind. Mind is the most fundamental ontological reality. This leads to the metaphysical position known as idealism.

According to metaphysicians, there are three fundamental ways we can view the universe. Dualists view the universe is made of two substances, mind and matter. As we learned in Part I, how do we account for the interaction between these two substances? How does mind affect matter and how does matter affect mind? Materialist are monists, saying that there is only one substance. That one substance is matter. However, as we learned in Part II, how does mind or consciousness or spirit arise from a world made of mere matter? In Part III we will consider a third possibility, known as idealism. Idealism teaches that at a fundamental level, everything is mind. The mental is the ultimate reality. Mind permeates everything that exists, an approach known as panpsychism.

Most modern philosophers reject Idealism as an approach to metaphysics. But as we will show, it is an idea with a long history. Hindu thinkers; Greek Neoplatonists; medieval mystics; Enlightenment thinkers such as Berkeley, Leibniz, and Kant; and modern philosophers such as Alfred North Whitehead all saw mind or consciousness as the ultimate reality. To dismiss it out hand is like a fish dismissing the existence of water out of hand. We live in a world so infused with consciousness or mind that we barely notice it. What does it mean to claim that mind is the ultimate reality?

In the East

Some of the most ancient philosophical writings began in India, with the Vedas, containing hymns and praises to the various gods. Chanting the

Vedas is a central ritual in the ancient religions of India known as Hinduism. (I use the plural deliberately, because Hinduism, a term that simply means the religion of India, contains multiple, sometimes contradictory positions.) For our purposes, perhaps the most important of the Vedas was a section known as the Upanishads.

The Upanishads contain some of the most fundamental religious ideas in Hinduism. At the center of these ideas is *Brahman*, the ultimate reality from whence everything comes and to whence everything returns. Many Hindus may believe and worship a variety of gods, but all of these gods ultimately are manifestations of *Brahman*. The three major such gods are Brahma the creator, Vishnu the sustainer, and Shiva the destroyer. They are known as the *trimurti* or triumvirate of Hinduism. But at the core is *Brahman*, the fundamental reality behind each of these gods.

> Let me quote one of these Vedas to give a taste of idealistic thinking in early Hinduism: There was neither non-existence nor existence then; there was neither the realm of space nor the sky which is beyond. What stirred? Where? In whose protection? Was there water, bottomlessly deep? There was neither death nor immortality then. There was no distinguishing sign of night nor of day. That one breathed, windless, by its own impulse. Other than that there was nothing beyond. Darkness was hidden by darkness in the beginning; with no distinguishing sign, all this was water. The life force was covered with emptiness, that one arose through the power of heat. Desire came upon that one in the beginning; that was the first seed of mind.[2]

Although the quote is from the Vedas, a Jewish kabbalist could have written these words.

Humanity's individual selves are called *Atman*. These individual human souls are subject to *samsara*, the ongoing cycle of reincarnation. In this recycling of life and death, souls are reborn according to their *karma*, a kind of justice based on their behavior in previous lives. In fact, the entire Hindu caste system is based on this idea of *karma*, a person's actions in a previous life can affect their birth status in this life. A central theme of the great Hindu classic the *Bhagavad Gita* is *dharma*, the duties that we have based on the facts of our birth. Nonetheless, the ultimate goal is *moksha*, the eventual liberation from samsara, this seemingly unending cycle of death and rebirth.

Hindus believe that the world that exists around us is *maya*, an illusion. Everything is ultimately *Brahman*. In this Hindu vision of reality, *Brahman*

2. Doniger, *Norton Anthology*, "Big Veda" 10:129. 90.

is not exactly God as understood by theism in the West. In the West God is a person who has a will, and who acts according that that will. It would be incorrect to say that *Brahman* is a person or *Brahman* has a will. *Brahman* is simply the ultimate reality, the nature of things, from which everything else flows and to which everything returns.

This brings us to the main teaching of Hinduism. Everything, even our individual souls, is part of this ultimate reality. Hindus say *Atman is Brahman*. In Sanskrit the phrase is *Tat Tvam Asi*—"you are that." Our original pure self is not separated from all there is, but is part of that ultimate reality. If we were to identify *Brahman* with a universal mind, we could easily say that everything is mind. A soul is like a wave in the ocean, separate and yet part of the whole. When the wave reaches the shore it does not disappear, it simply becomes one with the water. Meditation become a way to connect to that universal mind. This idea will become important among mystics, not just in Eastern religions but in the West.

From Hinduism, it would be useful to turn to the other great religious tradition of India, Buddhism. My synagogue is located next door to the local Buddhist Temple. Our two houses of worship have a wonderful relationship. They allow us to use their parking lot on the High Holidays and we allow them to use our parking lot on Buddha's birthday. They brought us flowers on Rosh Hashanah. I have visited them and spoken with them. Often on Sunday morning as I say my prayers, I see people gathered in their parking lot doing meditation or practicing tai chi. In my relationship with the Buddhist Temple, I understand the appeal that this religion, whose roots are in India, has for so many Americans.

The roots of Buddhism are based on the teachings of Siddhartha Gautama, who lived in the fifth century BCE, known as the Buddha or enlightened one. Although raised in the Hindu tradition, Siddhartha traveled on a long journey to try to find the proper path. He was deeply troubled by the suffering he witnessed in the world. He eventually discovered what he considered the four noble truths. These truths are (1) life is suffering, (2) suffering is caused by desire, (3) the solution to suffering is to let go of desire, and (4) the way to let go of desire is to follow the eight-fold path. The Buddha taught that the things of this world are transitory and bound to disappear with time. Therefore, one should constantly strive to let go of the things of this world.

Buddhism does reject certain Hindu teachings such as the multiple gods, the priesthood and rituals, and perhaps most important, the caste system. However, Buddhism does accept other Buddhist teachings such as *samsara* and *karma*. The ultimate goal for a Buddhist is to reach a state known as *nirvana*, no longer part of this world but eternal bliss. There are various approaches to this within Buddhism. Some Buddhists believe that only monks and people who have made the maximum commitment to an ascetic life can reach *nirvana*. Others believe that *nirvana* is open to anyone. In fact, Mahayana Buddhism teaches that there are spiritual beings called bodhisattvas who, acting out of great compassion, delay their own passage to *nirvana* to help those here on earth.

Let me turn for a moment to one of the greatest differences between Hinduism and Buddhism. Hindus believe in *Atman*, our soul or spiritual essence, that survives death in order to be reincarnated into a new body. Such souls have a real existence. Buddhism teaches the principle of *anatta* or no-soul. On some ultimate level, our individual souls do not exist. To Buddhists, there are no essences, nothing that would cause cravings in this world.

It is intriguing to compare this Buddhist teaching to a Hassidic teaching of Dov Baer, the Maggid of Mezritch (1704–1772). It is doubtful that Dov Baer ever met a Buddhist in his life. But he taught that the Hebrew word for "I," *aniy*, has the same letters in Hebrew as the Hebrew word for "nothing"—*ayin*. To quote Dov Baer:

> Think of yourself as *ayin* and forget yourself totally. Then you can transcend time, rising to the world of thought, where all is equal: life and death, ocean and dry land. This is not the case when you are attached to the material nature of the world. If you think of yourself as something, God cannot be clothed in you, for God is infinite and no vessel can contain God—unless you think of yourself as *ayin*.[3]

The goal of meditation is to turn our self or soul into nothing. We see the importance of the cross-fertilization of ideas.

While looking at the East, let us turn for a moment to China, which developed its own religious traditions. The most important Chinese religions were Confucianism and Daoism. Buddhism eventually moved to China to become the third great Chinese religion. Of these three, Confucianism is the most practical, this worldly, concerned with behavior and obligation. In fact, many would claim that it is not a religion at all. It contains rituals and obligations toward parents, one's spouse, one's older brother, one's neighbor, and one's community. Of course, ancestor worship is also a vital part of Confucianism. Many have compared Confucius's book *The Analects* with Aristotle's *Nicomachean Ethics*. For example, both emphasize the middle way, the importance of moderation in one's behavior.

3. Quoted in Matt, *God and the Big Bang*, 75.

In a certain sense, Daoism is the opposite of Confucianism. It is other worldly, more concerned with flowing with the way, the ultimate nature of things. There is a spontaneity and a return to the nature of things in Daoism. Founded by Laozi, also known as Lao Tzu (605–531 BCE), Daoism is concerned with the nature of reality, the flow of things. The Dao or way must find the balance between the *yin* and the *yang*, often pictured as two parts of a circle, each leading into the other. At the beginning of Laozi's book the *Dao De Jing*, it says "The Dao which can be spoken is not the eternal Dao." The ultimate nature of things cannot be pinned down with words. This idea will become important when we study the mysticism of the West, where God's name cannot be spoken.

One of the great teachers of Daoism was Zhuangzi (370–287 BCE). Perhaps his most quoted saying is one he taught that when asleep, he dreamt that he was a butterfly. When he awoke, he said that he did not know if he was a man dreaming that he was a butterfly or a butterfly dreaming that he was a man. What we call reality seems unreal, even dream-like. The ultimate reality is in one's mind.

Idealism seems to be an excellent fit for Eastern culture. Hinduism, Buddhism, and Daoism all point toward the unreality of the material world. To Hindus this world is an illusion. To Buddhists this world is a place of clinging and desire, preventing one from reaching the otherworldly state of *nirvana*. To Daoists the goal is to live according to the spiritual way, separate from the practical life of the material world. Perhaps most telling is the Hindu idea that *Atman* is *Brahman*, our individual selves here in essence part of the ultimate reality. Idealism flourishes in the faith traditions of the East. But perhaps this belief in the transitory nature and non-reality of the material world is part of the reason that modern science grew up in the West, rather than the East. The West has a much more difficult time with idealism.

In the West

Idealism assumes that the material or physical world either has no reality or is at best a secondary phenomenon, mind is primary. The difficulty comes when you try to fit this in with the biblical creation story, the founding myth of Western thinking. If God created the heaven and the earth and God saw that they were very good, then how can we say that the universe has no material reality? Most Western thinkers are either dualists such as Descartes or Locke, or else materialists such as Hobbes or Marx. We have already looked at some of the difficulties of both dualism and materialism. Nonetheless, both assume an actual, physical or material world.

How can we reconcile the creation story in the West with idealism, the notion that mind is the ultimate reality? The answer lies in seeing emanation rather than creation as the ultimate act of God. God did not create a material universe outside himself. God is not separate from the universe. Rather, God is the ultimate mind, and God literally flowed into the universe. Everything that exists is part of God's very being. That is the meaning of the *Zohar*'s interpretation of the first lines of Genesis, which say that something, some ultimate reality, created God. God is the universe. Some such as Spinoza call this pantheism, the idea that God and nature are the same thing. And some such as the process philosophers call this panentheism, the idea that God is both within and beyond the universe. If God is mind and the universe is God, then the universe is mind. This is the kind of idealism that grew up in the West.

To understand the history of this idea, we must begin with Plato. Plato was a dualist; he believed in a material world of change and decay and an immaterial world of perfect forms. As we have already mentioned, the soul comes into this physical world from that world of the forms. Eventually it returns to the perfect place. The Western idea of heaven and eternal life grew out of these Platonic ideas. The physical world is real but secondary. We can use our mind to reach this ideal world. This is where Aristotle disagreed with his teacher Plato. To Aristotle there is no world of the forms, only this material world that we can study. To Aristotle, we learn of the world through our senses. As Aristotle taught, "there is nothing in the mind which is not first in the senses." Aristotle's ideas eventually developed into the modern philosophical idea of empiricism, that knowledge comes through the senses. Plato's ideas on the other hand eventually developed into the modern philosophical idea of rationalism, that knowledge comes through the mind.

Plato accepted the idea of spiritual realities beyond the material world that we can reach only through our mind. The greatest interpreter of Plato's works was the pagan philosopher Plotinus (204/5–270 CE). Roman by birth but living in Alexandria, Plotinus considered himself a Platonist. Later scholars, however, would use the term "Neoplatonism" to describe Plotinus's approach to reality. Plotinus's was an attempt to fill the void, creating spiritual realities that flowed from one to another. Plotinus built his entire system on divine emanation. Because of his importance in later mysticism, we will consider his work in some detail.

The best way to picture Plotinus's outlook is to imagine a multilevel punch bowl at a party. Punch flows from the higher to the lower levels, filling the levels below and eventually reaching the bottom level. Stephen MacKenna, in his introduction to his translation of Plotinus's *The Enneads*, gives a simple summary:

> The system of Plotinus is a system of necessary emanation, procession, or irradiation accompanied by necessary aspiration or reversion-to-source; all the forms and phases of Existence flow from the Divinity and all strive to return thither and remain there. This divinity is a graded Triad. Its three Hypostases—or in modern religious terminology, "persons"—are in the briefest description: 1. The One, or First Existent; 2. The Divine Mind, or First Thinker and Thought; 3. The All-Soul, or first and only principle of life. Of all things the governance and the existence are in these three.[4]

The highest level in Plotinus's vision is the One or the Good. The One is absolute unity, unknowable to the human mind. Plotinus compares the One to a spring that is the source of many rivers, but the spring is never diminished within itself: "Imagine a spring that has no source outside itself; it gives itself to all the rivers, yet is never exhausted by what they take, but remains always integrally as it was."[5] Plotinus teaches that the One is everywhere, but it is also nowhere. The One is everything, but it is also so unknowable that it is nothing.

Plotinus continues:

> How then does unity give rise to multiplicity? By its omnipresence: there is nowhere where it is not; it occupies therefore, all that is; at once, it is manifold—or, rather, it is all things. If it were simply and solely everywhere, all would be this one thing alone: but it is, also, in no place, and this gives, in the final result, that, while all exists by means of it, in virtue of its omnipresence, all is distinct from it, in virtue of its being nowhere.[6]

Plotinus's unique idea is that only an everything that is also a nothing can be both unified and the source of multiplicity.

The second stage in Plotinus's vision of emanation is the intelligence, using the Greek term *nous*. *Nous* is still one, but it contains the potential for many. As Plotinus put it:

4. Plotinus, *Enneads*, xxv–xxvi.

5. Plotinus, *Enneads*, 249.

6. Plotinus, *Enneads*, 253.

> The Highest began as a unity but did not remain as it began; all unknown to itself, it became manifold; it grew, as it were pregnant: desiring universal possession, it flung itself outward, though it were better had it never know the desire by which a Secondary came into being.[7]

If the first is considered One, the second can be considered One-Many. It is only with this second level that the potential for multiplicity exists. This is the world of the forms. But they are forms without material substance, a form without matter. (We should note that Aristotle would disagree with this idea, claiming that form without matter cannot exist.)

The third level is the region of the Soul, also known as the World Soul. This is the realm of the One and the Many, and it includes our individual souls. From this level, multiplicity and division enter the world. From the World Soul ultimately flows the world of matter, the real material world in which we live. Plotinus's goal is for our individual souls to leave the material world in which we dwell, and through meditation work our way back up to the One.

Here we have a different creation story from that of the philosophers such as the Muslim Avicenna, the Jewish Maimonides, and the Christian Thomas Aquinas, each of whom built their systems on the work of Aristotle. They saw a God as a creator and presumed an ontological gap between creator and creation. If the key idea for Maimonides was creation *ex nihilo*, the key idea for the Neoplatonists was emanation. Rather than creating a world outside himself, God literally flowed into the world. Neoplatonism allows for an immanent view of God. There is no gap between creator and creation. Neoplatonism would become extremely influential in the mystical traditions of Judaism, Christianity, and Islam. One can see the line of influence from Plotinus's the One, the nous, and the World Soul to Kabbalah's *Ein Sof* and the *sefirot*, which flow from it. Nonetheless, there is a major difference between Neoplatonism and kabbalah.

In Neoplatonism reality flows from the highest levels down to this world without an act of will or desire. It happens automatically, as a spring flows into brook. There is no will. Jewish Neoplatonists such as the great poet Ibn Gabirol (1021–1058) disagree, saying that there must be a will that begins this process of emanation. This will or desire becomes the first of the ten *sefirot* of classical kabbalah, known as *Keter*. Although the term *Keter* means "crown," most scholars usually translate it as "divine will." Perhaps this idea was best expressed by the contemporary Jewish philosopher and expert on Gnosticism, Hans Jonas (1903–1993):

7. Plotinus, *Enneads*, 246.

> In the beginning, for unknowable reasons, the ground of being,
> or the Divine, chose to give itself over to the chance and risk
> and endless variety of becoming. And wholly so: entering into
> the adventure of space and time, the deity held back nothing of
> itself: no uncommitted or unimpaired part remained to direct,
> correct, and ultimately guarantee the devious working-out of
> its destiny in creation. On this unconditional immanence the
> modern temper insists.[8]

Idealism in the West is most prominent in the various mystical traditions, including kabbalah, which grew out of Neoplatonism. We will look at
Jewish mysticism in greater detail in a later chapter. But mysticism is based
on the idea that there is an underlying reality and a unity to everything,
not unlike the Hindu idea of *Brahman*. In fact, some scholars claim that
Western mysticism grew partially through contact with Eastern religions.
The material world is, if not an illusion, then something that one can escape
from proper mystical practices. The goal of the mystic is to reunite with the
unity. The world is filled with the mind of God.

In Modern Philosophy

Modern philosophy began with the end of the scholastic age, the beginning
of the scientific revolution, and the philosophy of Rene Descartes (1596–
1650). As already mentioned, Descartes was a rationalist and a dualist. He
proved that the mind exists, and went on to prove the body exists. Mind
and body are two separate substances: mind is *res cogitans* (a thinking substance) and body is a *res extensa* (an extended thing), something that takes
up space. Two other classical rationalist philosophers, Benedict Spinoza
(1632–1677) and Gottfried Leibniz (1646–1716), would bring two different
types of idealism into the modern age.

Spinoza taught that there was only one substance, and everything that
exists are modes of that one substance. Mind and matter are both manifestations of that one underlying substance. As Spinoza put it, *deus sive natura*—
"God is nature." Spinoza was a pantheist who taught that the entire natural
world is simply God. The material world and God are one. For such radical
ideas, Spinoza was excommunicated at the age of twenty-three from the
synagogue and cut off from his Jewish community. Personally, I think it is
time for Jews to reclaim this brilliant philosopher. Centuries after Spinoza,
when Einstein was asked if he believed in God, he responded, "I believe in
Spinoza's God."

8. Jonas, *Mortality and Morality*, 134.

Leibniz also accepted the Aristotle's classical idea of substance. But instead of only one substance, Leibniz saw a world made up of countless individual substances. Each of these individual substances had its own mind and each acted independently of all the others. Leibniz named these substances monads. Each monad is unaware of the workings of every other monad. And yet they all work together in what Leibniz called a "pre-established harmony," which we discussed earlier in the chapter on dualism. Supposedly Leibniz once traveled to Holland and met with Spinoza. I would love to be a fly on the wall during that meeting.

By each of these monads working together, God was able to make this into "the best of all possible world." Voltaire mocked Leibniz and his philosophy in his classic novel *Candide*. Nonetheless, Leibniz's ideas would centuries later become the basis of Alfred North Whitehead's process philosophy, probably the most serious attempt to come up with a philosophy in keeping with both idealism and modern science. We will look at Whitehead later in this chapter.

Turning from the rationalists who taught that knowledge comes from the mind, let us turn to the empiricists, who taught that knowledge comes from the senses. If rationalists were centered in continental Europe, empiricists were centered in Great Britain. The first modern empiricist was John Locke (1632–1704.) Locke taught that our mind is a *tabula rasa*—"a blank slate" that imprints information it receives from the world. There are primary qualities from the physical world such as shape, size, and motion. Then there are secondary qualities created by the mind such as color, sound, and taste. Obviously to Locke there is a real world out there, so Locke was a dualist. But what was important is that the mind contains no innate ideas, it is written on by the outside world.

The empiricist thinker who took Locke's ideas to an extreme was George Berkeley (1685–1753). Berkeley became the chief proponent of idealism. He was opposed to the materialism of his age. He taught that for something to exist, it must be sensed within the mind. In fact, he specifically taught *esse is percipi*—"to exist is to be perceived." All existence must take place in a mind. According to a famous story of the time, the philosopher Samuel Johnson kicked a stone, felt the pain in his foot, and said, "I disprove Berkeley thus." Unfortunately for Johnson, this did not disprove Berkeley. The pain he felt in his foot was perceived by his mind.

One could ask the question following Berkeley, do material things disappear when there is no one there to perceive them? If I leave my office, does my desk no longer exist? Berkeley's answer is that God has a mind that perceives everything. In fact, for Berkeley this was proof of the existence of God. Berkeley's answer about God or a universal mind also answers one of the fundamental questions of idealism. If everything is mind, I know my mind exists but how do I know other minds exist? If to exist is to be perceived, is not my mind the one doing the perceiving? What about other minds? This philosophical problem is called solipsism. The simple answer is that the mind of God exists and all our individual minds are part of God's mind. This appears to be a Western version of the Hindu idea *Atman* is *Brahman*.

The most important of the empiricists who built on Berkeley's work was the Scotsman David Hume (1711–1776). Hume, like Locke and Berkeley, believed that knowledge comes from the senses. But he was deeply skeptical about what we can know. We have already seen his skepticism in previous chapters on miracles and the problem of evil. Hume taught that we cannot know causality (that there is a causal connection between events); without causality the basis of determinism is undermined. He also questioned whether we can know anything by inductive reasoning. (Because the sun rose every day in the past, how do we know it will rise tomorrow?) He said we cannot know ethics by looking out into the world. (He taught that "you cannot learn an ought from an is." All ethics are just sentiments.)

In fact, there are only two things we can know for sure. We can know statements that are true by definition or through logic, which he called analytic statements. And we can know statements that are true because we learn them from our senses, what he called synthetic statements. Everything else is unknowable, what later empiricists would call nonsense. One of Hume's most colorful quotes says:

> If we take in our hand any volume; of divinity or school metaphysics, for instance. Let us ask, does it contain any abstract reasoning concerning quantity or number? No [analytic statements]. Does it contain any experimental reasoning concerning matter of fact and existence? No [synthetic statements]. Commit it then to the flames, for it can contain nothing but sophistry and illusion.[9]

Philosophers call this dichotomy between two kinds of ideas Hume's Fork.

Hume taught that there exists very little our minds can know—we cannot know causality, induction, ethics, miracles, or theology for that matter. Hume was an atheist and even on his deathbed his friends could not convince him to profess a faith in God. If we only read Hume, we would give up on knowing much of anything. But fortunately, Hume philosophy provoked a reaction from the man I consider the greatest idealistic philosopher of them all, Immanuel Kant. We have already encountered Kant's categorical

9. Hume, *Enquiry*, 86.

imperative in our chapter on ethics. Now we must turn to Kant's theory of knowledge and his attempt to combine rationalism and empiricism into a revolutionary new philosophy.

From Kant to Hegel

Immanuel Kant (1724–1804) was a man of habit. He lived his entire life in his native Konigsberg and locals would say they could set their watches by the time he took his daily walk. Kant claimed that he read Hume and it "awoke me from my dogmatic slumber." In his *Critique of Pure Reason*, Kant came up with an idealistic philosophy that revolutionized how we see the world. I tell my philosophy students that I believe Kant's ideas directly led to Einstein.

Kant called his philosophy a Copernican revolution. Copernicus had gone from a geocentric to a heliocentric view of the universe, from earth in the center to the sun in the center. In a similar matter, Kant developed a philosophy that says we see the world not from a God's eye point of view but from the view of our individual minds. Kant called this move "the turn to subject." There may be a material world out there, what Kant called the noumenal world, but we can never know it. We can only know how our individual minds see the world, what Kant called the phenomenal world.

Our minds are built so that we see the world in a certain way. There is a priori knowledge built into our mind. In fact, when we spoke about synthetic statements as being based on our senses, Kant said that there are also "a priori synthetic" statements, statements built into the very nature of our minds. For example, our minds perceive events in the world in terms of time and space. Newton had said that time and space are absolutes that exist in the universe. Kant disagreed; we can never know if time and space exist in the real world, but time and space do exist in our minds, in the way we see the world. So too the idea of substance. We do not know if substances really exist in the outside world. (In fact, the desk I am writing on is made up of atoms that are mostly empty space, having no real substance in and of themselves.) But we see the world in terms of substance; I sense the desk as something solid. Causality may not exist in the noumenal world as Hume taught. But causality exists in the phenomenal world of our mind. We see causality in the world. Kant used the phrase "a priori synthetic" for the categories of how our mind organizes knowledge.

Kant's philosophy goes by the name transcendental idealism. Kant does not deny that there is a world out there. But he claims that the world in itself, what Kant called *das ding an sich*, is unknown to us. All we can know is what our mind sees, how our mind organizes the world. Later thinkers would build on Kant by removing the notion of a world out there altogether. The only world is the world of our minds. This centrality of mind will become crucial in a later chapter when we look at relativity and particularly quantum physics. Both are based on the denial of a God's eye view of the world, but rather the world as seen by an observer. That is why I claim that Kant led directly to Einstein.

Kant began an entire movement, often called German idealism, which taught that the mind was the ultimate reality and it was mind that moved through history. This movement was often tied to romanticism, which was a reaction to the intellectual approach of the Enlightenment that sought to analyze everything and was overly rational. We will look at romanticism in further detail in the next chapter. Again, we see in this German idealism the interplay with Daoism. One of most prominent of these German idealists was Arthur Schopenhauer (1788–1860). Schopenhauer wrote *The World as Will and Representation*. The mind represents the world outside and acts through the will inside. Schopenhauer was one of the few idealistic philosophers who explicitly studied Eastern philosophy and acknowledged his debt to Eastern faiths, particularly Buddhism.

There are numerous other German idealists worthy of mention, such as Johann Gottlieb Fichte (1762–1814) and Friedrich Wilhelm Joseph Schelling (1775–1854). Perhaps the most influential was Georg Wilhelm Friedrich Hegel (1770–1831). Hegel was an absolute idealist who taught that *geist* "mind or spirit" is dynamic and works its way out through human history. He claimed that Kant's view of the mind was too static. Hegel worked out his famous dialectic, where thesis is confronted by antithesis and then resolved by synthesis. The synthesis becomes a new thesis, confronted by a new antithesis, and resolved again by a new synthesis. This dynamic history of spirit and the three-part dialectic is very close to inner dynamism between the various *sefirot* in the kabbalah. Some scholars speculate that Hegel studied kabbalah.

Eventually Western philosophy rejected this German idealism in favor of materialism, existentialism, and perhaps most influential in the early twentieth century, logical empiricism. The logical empiricists, centered around the Vienna Circle before World War II, claimed that the only legitimate statements were those that can be verified. Since statements about mind are subjective and cannot be verified, they are illegitimate. The world of philosophy moved beyond Hegel.

Nonetheless, with the fading of German idealism, mind as the ultimate reality was not dead. This period saw the growth of psychology, a new area of science that broke off from philosophy. Certainly Sigmund Freud

(1856–1939), one of the great minds of modern thoughts, was a materialist. He taught the importance of the unconscious mind as a source of drives and of frequent neurotic behavior. But it was Freud's student Carl Jung (1875–1961) who introduced the idea of a collective unconscious.

Carl Jung was one of Freud's most devoted followers. In fact, Freud saw himself as a father-figure to the younger Jung. Freud also saw the importance of having Jung who was not Jewish as a follower of psychoanalysis so that in the anti-Semitic climate of Europe at that time, psychoanalysis would not be considered a Jewish science. Therefore, it was extremely painful to both men when Jung broke with Freud. They differed on many issues, but one of the most important was religion. Whereas Freud totally rejected religion, Jung saw a positive value in religion.

Jung believed in a collective unconscious, a kind of idealism. People shared certain unconscious ideas not because of some mystical connection between their brains but because of similarity of brain structures. Whereas Freud believed the unconscious was something filled with repressed, negative content, Jung saw it as much more neutral. Certain symbols and images, which Jung called archetypes, filled this collective unconscious. Religious ideas such as water as a symbol of rebirth or light as a symbol of creation were present across various cultures and religions.

Idealism has its followers today. The idea that mind is the ultimate reality is vital both in modern science and in classical mysticism. One thinker who tried to revive the idea was Alfred North Whitehead (1861–1947), founder of process philosophy. I wrote my PhD dissertation on Whitehead's thought, using it to interpret the creation story in the *Zohar*. Let me end this chapter with a brief summary of Whitehead's thinking.

Process Philosophy

What is the ultimate reality? Whitehead rejects the materialistic image, popular among scientists, that reality consists of inert bits of matter moved by external forces. Rather, he offers an image of reality somewhat similar to Leibniz's monads. Reality is built of bits of mind or experience. Whitehead calls these fundamental bits of reality "actual occasions" or "actual entities."

Each of these actual entities is vanishingly small, exists for a very short duration of time, then vanishes. But, while each is alive, it is under the influence of all the other actual entities in the universe. It is also under the influence of, what Whitehead calls, "eternal objects." And, when each actual entity vanishes, it becomes the basis of a new generation of actual entities. It is this interplay of actual entities, influencing one another, changing, vanishing while influencing the next generation of such entities, that White-head calls his "philosophy of organism." To quote Whitehead:

> "Actual entities"—also termed "actual occasions"—are the final real things of which the world is made up. There is no going behind actual entities to find anything more real. They differ among themselves: God is an actual entity, and so is the most trivial puff of existence in far-off empty space. But, though there are gradations of importance, and diversities of function, yet in the principles which actuality exemplifies all are on the same level. The final facts are, all alike, actual entities; and these actual entities are drops of experience, complex and interdependent.[10]

Whitehead uses the term *prehension* to describe how each actual entity comprehends all other actual entities, then creatively moves forward to influence future entities. He goes into some detail about this prehension. First, Whitehead teaches that each actual entity has a physical pole in space. Through this physical pole, it is able to grasp or take within itself every other actual entity currently in existence. Whitehead sees this as a one-way process, with actual entities grasping previous actual entities but previous actual entities not prehending new ones. He uses the mathematical term *vector* to indicate this one-way movement. The past can affect the present, but the present cannot affect the past. Time and process are interwoven, for Whitehead. The future is open-ended. There is forward causation but no backward causation.

Each actual entity also has a mental pole. Through this pole, the entity prehends what Whitehead calls "eternal objects." They exist as pure potentiality. In a sense, these eternal objects can be compared to Platonic forms that are reflected in the substances of this world. Each actual entity prehends these eternal objects and either accepts or rejects them. "The eternal object is always a potentiality for actual entities; but in itself, as conceptually felt, it is neutral as to the fact of its physical ingression in any particular actual entity of the temporal world."[11]

Bringing together the various actual occasions and the relevant eternal objects is a process that Whitehead calls "concrescence," from the word "concrete." It works very much like human consciousness, which combines sensations, memories, decisions, feelings, and various impressions, below the level of consciousness, and then makes a decision how to proceed. So each actual entity brings together both other actual entities and the eternal

---

10. Whitehead, *Process and Reality*, 18.

11. Whitehead, *Process and Reality*, 70.

forms in a concrete way. This decision of how to proceed is where creativity enters the picture.

Finally, each actual occasion has a subjective aim. Many process philosophers use the word "lure," the direction in which it wants to go. This is the final cause or teleology we mentioned earlier. The actual occasion pulls together the input in its physical pole (other actual entities), the input in its mental pole (eternal objects), its subjective aim, and creatively moves forward. Whitehead calls this step "satisfaction." The many aspects come together to become one movement: "The many become one, and are increased by one. In their natures, entities are disjunctively 'many' in process of passage into conjunctive unity."[12] And when it becomes one, the actual entity vanishes and ceases to exist as a subject. It now becomes, what Whitehead calls, a superject—an object for the next generation of actual entities. "An actual entity is at once the subject experiencing and the superject of its experiences. It is subject-superject, and neither half of this description can for a moment be lost sight."[13]

Whitehead's theology has not been influential among philosophers. What has been influential is his image of God among theologians. Whitehead imagined a three-part God, but not the trinity of Christian thought. God is an actual entity. Like every actual entity, God has both a mental pole and a physical pole. The mental pole is that through which an entity prehends eternal objects. In the temporal world, an actual entity only prehends some eternal objects; God, however, prehends all eternal objects. Whitehead calls this mental pole that contains all eternal objects the primordial nature of God. Like the physical pole of all actual entities, the physical pole of God prehends all actual entities in the universe. Everything that happens. This is a God that is constantly in process, constantly changing as a result of his relationship with the world. Whitehead calls this the consequent nature of God.

Finally, as we described above, every actual entity is both a subject and a superject. As subject, it prehends both eternal objects and other actual entities. Through concrescence, it brings these together into a new form. It then passes away but, in so doing, it becomes the superject, the object of future actual entities. God, however, does not pass away. But since God is also a superject, and becomes the subjective aim of every actual entity, this description leads to an image of God who uses persuasion rather than coercion.

12. Whitehead, *Process and Reality*, 21.

13. Whitehead, *Process and Reality*, 29.

I have found a simple metaphor to clarify these ideas. Metaphors are not meant to be true or false. They are either useful or not useful. This metaphor is useful to me. I imagine Whitehead's God like a GPS (global positioning system) device. I have a GPS in my car and another in my phone. From the beginning, it contains much information—maps, streets, locations I use regularly, and weather information. They are there as potential for my use, even before I turn on the GPS. This is comparable to the primordial nature of God. Then I turn on my GPS and enter basic information, my current location and desired destination. Perhaps it will also take into consideration construction or traffic patterns. It takes in new information and adjusts itself accordingly. This is the consequent nature of God. Then, my GPS digests all this information and tells me which way to go. "Turn right at the next street." This is the superject nature of God. I can follow the GPS's instructions or I can ignore them, and go straight instead of turning right. The GPS does not coerce me. And when I go down a different path, the GPS says "recalculating." I love the image of God constantly saying, about the world, "recalculating."

What I love about Whitehead's admittedly complicated description of the world is how he envisions mind permeating everything. Each of these minds has free will. God may give them an aim, but they are free to choose to follow or not follow, just as I am free to follow my GPS in my car or not. God becomes a God of persuasion rather than coercion. And the universe slowly evolves toward some ideal, step-by-step, lured on by God. It is a powerful image. But how close is it to the modern scientific view of the world? In the next chapter we will explore nature, and ask the question whether soul or spirit permeates nature. Then in the subsequent chapter by looking at God's first act of creation—what is light?

CHAPTER 9

Nature—Does the Universe Have a Soul?

A scorpion once asked a frog if he could climb on the frog's back and get a ride across a river. The frog replied, "Are you crazy? You will sting me and I will die." The scorpion replied, "If I sting you and you die, then I will fall into the river and drown." The frog was convinced and told the scorpion to get on his back. Halfway across the river the frog suddenly felt a sting. The frog cried out, "Why did you do that? Now we will both die." The scorpion wistfully said, "I could not help it. It is in my nature."

I first heard this story in the 1992 movie *The Crying Game* and have used it in sermons ever since. The movie, nominated for the Best Picture Academy Award, tells the story of an Irish Republican Army member Fergus who meets a prisoner they have captured, and decides to make a play for the prisoner's girlfriend, Dil. Dil is portrayed as a beautiful woman. About halfway through the movie Fergus (and the movie audience) discovers that Dil is not a woman at all but a man. It is one of the earliest films I can remember that deals with transgender issues. The actor Jaye Davidson was nominated for an Academy Award as best supporting actor for his portrayal of Dil. (The fact that he was nominated as an actor rather than an actress gives away an important part of the plot.)

The story makes sense within the entire argument today about transgender issues. Are we limited by our nature? Or can we transcend our nature? What is the ontological status of nature itself? Or to put it most simply, does nature have a soul?

Is Nature Alive?

When I was a child my parents sent me to a beautiful summer camp in the mountains of Northern California. Some of my favorite memories took place in that camp. Although many Jews went there, the camp was not Jewish. Nor was it Christian. Nonetheless, the camp owners felt that the weekly schedule ought to include a spiritual experience for campers and staff. Each Sunday night after dinner, we went out on the grass in the meadow and had Sunday night vespers. I will admit that I had no idea what the word "vespers" meant. But that Sunday night spiritual moment is one of my favorite memories of the camp.

We were out in nature, in sight of the forests and mountains as the sun was setting. The weather was often cool. Deer would sometimes graze at the very edge of the meadow. We would sing songs, recite poems, and reflect on the spiritual meaning of life, as best children can. There was a sense that all around us, nature was alive. As an adult, I have often enjoyed connecting nature to my religious observance. I have put on a tallit, wrapped tefillin, and recited the morning prayers from the top of Masada, watching the sun rise over the Dead Sea. I have recited my morning prayers on the beach, on the edge of the Grand Canyon, on a mountain top, and in the forest. There are moments when nature seems alive with spirit.

Of course, intellectually I know that nature is not necessarily so spiritual. Would I feel such spirit at the edge of a swamp, with mosquitos buzzing about? Would I feel the same way about praying at the ocean if a tsunami was coming? What about on a mountain top if it was a volcano about to blow? Nature can be beautiful, but nature can also be cruel.

Nonetheless, there is a long tradition of seeing nature as somehow alive. The ancient pagans were nature worshippers. The religion they practiced was called animism, a religion that saw nature as infused with spirit. Edward Tylor (1832–1917), one of the earliest anthropologists of religion, taught that it is the nature of humans to see spirit in everything. Animals, trees, even rocks are infused with consciousness. These ancient pagan ideas have often been translated into modern literature. One thinks of the mother tree in Disney's *Pocahontas* giving comfort and advice to the young Indian princess. Tylor taught that belief in animism was part of human nature. We see the natural world as alive; why else would we give a name to a hurricane and describe its behavior as if it has a will of its own. I heard people say in 1992, "Hurricane Andrew decided to turn south, sparing Miami Beach."

Paganism was the popular religion of the ancient world. An important part of pagan thinking was the worship of nature. Spirit was seen in everything, and those spirits must be influenced to bring about good crops, offer healing, or protect the community. Often there were sacrifices to assuage what people thought were angry spirits. Pagans had a cyclical view of religion, tied to the cycles of nature. The day, the month or full cycle of the moon, the year or full cycle of the earth around the sun, were tied to worship. The beginning of the book of Ecclesiastes, although part of the Hebrew Bible, reflected this cyclical thinking: "That which has been is what shall be, and that which has been done is what shall be done. There is nothing new under the sun" (Ecclesiastes 1:9).

To the pagan world, life is an endless cycle. The philosopher Friedrich Nietzsche, who had little use for Judaism and even less for Christianity, wrote about the importance of an eternal recurrence. Everything that happens will come back and happen again. The symbol of this worldview was the circle. We will explore Nietzsche's thought in greater detail later in this chapter.

In many ways, the Abrahamic religions of the West were a reaction to this early paganism. The Hebrew Bible cut through this pagan view like a ray of light. Life is more like a line than a circle. History has a direction. Abraham is told to leave his home, enter a new land, and build a new life different from the one of his childhood. Moses leads the ancient Israelites from slavery to freedom. Isaiah shares a vision of a Messianic future, a time of peace and prosperity. The future will be better than the present. We can change. The Irish writer Thomas Cahill called this image of the line *The Gifts of the Jews* in his powerful book. To quote Cahill:

> All evidence points to there having been, in the earliest religious thought, a vision of the cosmos that was profoundly cyclical. . . . The Jews were the first people to break out of this circle, to find a new way of thinking and experiencing, a new way of understanding and feeling the world, so much so that it may be said with some justice that theirs is the only new idea that human beings have ever had.[1]

Despite this emphasis on a linear view of the world that was an essential part of Western religion, the pagan view never truly died out. It has come back in contemporary times through various pagan religions such

1. Cahill, *Gifts of the Jews*, 5.

as Wiccan, Druid, and various return to nature movements. Often these religions go by the name neopaganism. Ethan Doyle White describes these movements as "a collection of modern religious, spiritual, and magical traditions that are self-consciously inspired by the pre-Judaic, pre-Christian, and pre-Islamic belief systems of Europe, North Africa, and the Near East."[2] Many of the rites of these modern movements are directly linked to the cycles of nature, with special observances at the full moon or during the summer and winter solstice and spring and fall equinox.

Western religion rejected the animism of the ancient pagans. It saw nature as God's creation, but not as something holy and animated within itself. As we learned earlier, according to classical theism God was wholly separated from nature. God could manipulate nature. This ontological gap between God and nature allowed the scientific revolution to blossom, often with an extremely instrumental view of nature. Humans tried to understand nature in order to utilize her for their own purposes. Francis Bacon, in many ways the intellectual founder of the scientific revolution, famously said, "Let the human race recover that right over nature which belonged to it by divine bequest, and let power be given it; the exercise thereof will be governed by sound reason and true religion."[3] Nature was utterly passive. Of course, not everybody agreed. Spinoza had written that not only was nature animated by spirit, nature was spirit. *Deus sive natura*—"nature is God." But it was the Romantics at the end of the eighteenth and beginning of the nineteenth century who truly envisioned a return to the spirit of nature.

Romanticism

Romanticism was a movement in poetry, art, music, as well as philosophy, which grew in the late eighteenth and early nineteenth centuries. Many see it as a reaction against the rationalism and instrumentalism of the early Enlightenment. Romanticism was often marked by a return to emotions. One only needs to compare the music of Mozart, with its precise classical structure, to the music of the latter Beethoven, with its sweeping passion, to get a feel for this age. One also sees the power of emotions in the poetry of William Wordsworth. Romantics saw nature as something to be approached not for its utility as early scientists saw it, but as something that appeals to the emotions.

To many of these romantics, the founder was the philosopher Jean-Jacques Rousseau (1712–1778). Rousseau famously wrote, "Man is born

2. E. D. White, *Wicca*, 6.

3. Bacon, *Novum Organon*, 301.

free and everywhere is in chains." Rousseau's words, although influential in the French Revolution, were meant to signify how civilization had corrupted humanity by destroying his natural self. Babies should be raised in nature. Rousseau would have appreciated the modern treatment given to his ideas in such literary works as Rudyard Kipling's *The Jungle Book* and Edgar Rice Burroughs's *The Legend of Tarzan*. Rousseau sought to reform education so that children are raised within nature, not corrupted by civilization.

Romanticism saw nature as having a deep intrinsic value that had been lost by the rationalism and instrumentalism of the Enlightenment. Nature did not simply exist for human utility but had a value of its own. Humans needed to unleash their emotions and live lives more in tune with nature. These ideas also took hold in America through what is often called the transcendental movement. Such thinkers as Ralph Waldo Emerson (1803–1882) and Henry David Thoreau (1817–1862) taught self-reliance and living lives at one with nature. Thoreau tried to describe the life of simplicity he built for himself at Walden Pond. The transcendentalists believed that culture had corrupted the purity of individuals, who ought to return to nature. Transcendentalists had a core belief in the goodness of nature as opposed to the corruption of society.

In Europe, many of these ideas would influence the powerful German philosopher Friedrich Nietzsche (1844–1900). Nietzsche was not really a romantic but rather an early existentialist thinker. Still, he thought that European culture had destroyed the soul of modern Europeans. To Nietzsche, God was dead and Christian morality was a slave morality. It was time for a person to reject European civilization and rather create himself as an *ubermensch*—a strong, independent, self-reliant human being. If God is dead, that people should become as gods.

It was Nietzsche who most passionately called for a return to ancient paganism. He differentiated between the two sons of Zeus, Apollo and Dionysus. Apollo was the god of rationality while Dionysus was the god of wine and passion. Since the days of Socrates, Western thought had been Apollonian—overly rational and careful. It was time to reject Apollonian thinking in order to return to a Dionysian outlook, living by passions. Emotions rather than reason were more important. Nietzsche believed that the life of the passions was necessary because of his doctrine of eternal return. We will be forced to live our lives over and over again. We may as well live according to our passions. Nietzsche clearly calls for a return to paganism along with a rejection of Jewish and Christian values. Humans are part of nature and ought to live in keeping with human nature.

These ideas of returning to nature and living by one's passions diminished toward the end of the nineteenth century. According to the logical positivists, the prominent philosophical movement of that age, only what-ever was verifiable was considered valid. One could not verify that nature has a soul. But ideas never totally die out. Today, encouraged by modern ecology and back to earth movements, this idea that the universe has a soul is coming back full force.

Modern Ecology

When I teach my philosophy class, I often begin the section on environ-mental awareness with a thought question. I ask my students: Suppose you were the only person left on earth. When you die there will be no more humans. And suppose there is only one tree left on earth. Would it be ethical to cut down that last tree for your use? Some see no problem with cutting down the tree, after all, there will be no humans left to enjoy it. Others see a problem, that the tree has a right to exist even if there are no people. The answer to this question shows how anthropocentric my class is. Does nature exist for humanity's use, or does nature have an intrinsic value even without humans? This question is at the heart of the ecological awareness that has flourished over the last several decades.

The beginning of greater ecological awareness was the publication of Rachel Carson's book *Silent Spring* (1962). It was a warning about envi-ronment destruction occurring on earth due to human industrial activity. Although taking on the chemical industry in particular, Carson expressed a concern of how water and air pollution were destroying the environment for humanity. Meanwhile, Paul Ehrlich's book *The Population Bomb* (1968) raised issues already discussed long ago by Thomas Malthus, that the popu-lation of humanity was growing at too great a rate for the earth's resources. These books began a movement to pointing out the dangers humanity presents to the natural world. It is an awareness even more prevalent today with concerns about the destruction of the rain forest, the ozone layers, and animal species, as well as the very real threat of global warning.

It was medieval historian Lynn Townsend White Jr. (1907–1987) who brought forward the religious roots of this growing ecological crisis. In a seminal 1966 essay, "The Historical Roots of Our Ecologic Crisis," White blamed the Christian interpretation of the biblical creation story for our ecological problems. To quote White:

> Especially in its Western form, Christianity is the most anthro-pocentric religion the world has seen. . . . Man shares, in great measure, God's transcendence of nature. Christianity, in abso-lute contrast to ancient paganism and Asia's religions (except,

perhaps, Zoroastrianism), not only established a dualism of man and nature but also insisted that it is God's will that man exploit nature for his proper ends.[4]

White goes on to describe ancient animism, and the changes made in the middle ages by Christian thought:

> At the level of the common people this worked out in an interesting way. In antiquity every tree, every spring, every stream, every hill had its own genius loci, its guardian spirit. These spirits were accessible to men, but were very unlike men; centaurs, fauns, and mermaids show their ambivalence. Before one cut a tree, mined a mountain, or dammed a brook, it was important to placate the spirit in charge of that particular situation, and to keep it placated. By destroying pagan animism, Christianity made it possible to exploit nature in a mood of indifference to the feelings of natural objects.[5]

White recommended a radically new way of understanding Christianity. He based his teaching on Francis of Assisi, known as St. Francis in the Catholic tradition, the founder of the Franciscans. Francis taught some rather radical ideals including the value of all God's creatures in God's eyes. To quote White once again, "Francis tried to depose man from his monarchy over creation and set up a democracy of all God's creatures."[6] I recall doing a program called the blessings of the pets at a Friday night service. I was looking for an appropriate blessing and could find nothing in Jewish tradition. Then I turned to Francis of Assisi. Part of his prayer goes, "We ask you to bless the animals and all living creatures. By the power of your love, enable them to live according to your plan. May we always praise you for all your beauty in creation."

White calls for a Christianity based not on exploitation of nature but rather stewardship of nature. He believes that this is much closer to the authentic biblical teaching as interpreted by Francis. Judaism has a similar call for stewardship in the midrash:

> At the time when the Holy One, Blessed be He, created the first man, he took him and led him around all the trees in the Garden of Eden. Look how beautiful and praiseworthy every one is. And everything I created, I created for you. Be careful not to corrupt

---

4. L. White, "Historical Roots."

5. L. White, "Historical Roots."

6. L. White, "Historical Roots."

or destroy my world. For if you destroy it, there is none to repair it after you.[7]

This is a beautiful passage that rabbis concerned with the environment like to quote. But it is still extremely anthropocentric. Nature was made for the sake of humanity, and therefore humanity must avoid anything that will destroy nature. Humanity was given the responsibility of stewardship over nature so nature will be protected for the sake of humanity. To many in the environmentalist movement this does not go far enough. Nature has a purpose for its own sake, beyond the needs of humanity.

Norwegian mountaineer and philosopher Arne Naess (1912–2009) coined the phrase "deep ecology" in a 1972–1973 paper. He contrasted it with "shallow ecology," which remains anthropocentric, seeking to care for the environment for the sake of humanity. In deep ecology, nature itself has rights. Naess goes beyond Peter Singer's idea of animal rights, to the idea that nature itself is an organism deserving rights. It is a holistic view of the natural world. Everything that exists is interrelated. Humans are part of nature as are all animals, and are thus deserving of rights. But the key issue is that all of nature is interconnected, all is an organism, and all has a right to fulfill its purpose. All life, human and nonhuman, has a right to flourish and have its well-being protected. Humans can do this by seeking to have minimal impact on the environment. This includes living lightly on the earth. To accomplish this, humans should also try to lower population. The idea that all of nature is a single organism with rights is a radical new idea.

The problem with deep ecology is that it can quickly deteriorate into misanthropy, seeing humanity as evil and destructive. Some would call humans "a cancer upon the earth." To quote one writer:

> Human happiness, and certainly human fecundity, are not as important as a wild and healthy planet. I know social scientists who remind me that people are part of nature, but it isn't true. Somewhere along the line—at about a billion years ago, maybe half that—we quit the contract and became a cancer. We have become a plague upon ourselves and upon the Earth. It is cosmically unlikely that the developed world will choose to end its orgy of fossil-energy consumption, and the Third World its suicidal consumption of landscape. Until such time as Homo sapiens should decide to rejoin nature, some of us can only hope for the right virus to come along.[8]

7. *Ecclesiastes Rabbah* on 7:11.
8. Graber, "Mother Nature."

To hope for a virus to wipe out humanity so that nature can flourish is the stuff of science fiction and B movies. It shows where any idea taken to an extreme can become destructive. I prefer to see the role of humans not as destroyers of nature but rather as repairers of nature.

It is no coincidence that new neopaganism has flourished around the same time as this deep ecology movement. There is a direct line from ancient paganism to the romanticism of the Enlightenment age to contemporary deep environmentalism. All see nature as alive, and like any other living creature, worthy of rights. All are built around the worship of nature. In a way, aspects of this fit into classical Judaism, which sees nature as God's creation and therefore "good." In fact, the Torah says God's creation is "very good." Very good but not perfect. And that brings me to how I, as a rabbi, must view nature.

Perfecting Nature

When my daughter gave birth to my grandson, a lactation nurse met with her in the hospital. This woman was passionate about the centrality of breast feeding as the most natural and therefore healthiest way to nourish a baby. I enjoyed talking with this young nurse, and I appreciated her passion. In fact, I shared with her the Talmudic passage I quoted at the beginning of the chapter on miracles, about the man who miraculously began to breastfeed his baby. There was only one problem. To this young woman, the natural way was the only way. Nature trumped everything else.

My daughter tried to nurse. Like so many women, she had difficulty, and after a brief time switched to formula. If I had known how expensive formula is, I might have pushed her to try nursing longer. But when my grandson switched to formula rather than mother's milk, he flourished. He was able to get the nutrition he needed. Sometimes the natural way is not the best way; sometimes we need to move beyond nature.

There is a movement today to prevent vaccinations. Many of the people involved with that movement are the same people who are pushing nursing as the only natural way. Vaccinations are not natural, and at least from the point of view of this group, dangerous. Many claim that vaccinations cause autism, something that has never been scientifically proven. But there is a philosophy behind this movement, one that teaches that what is natural is what is important, and we ought not to play with natural.

I can certainly understand the desire to eat natural foods, or to eat meat that has been raised in a more natural setting, free range rather than locked in a stockade. Avoiding cruelty to animals is a fundamental ethical value. Having said that, natural foods are often much more subject to natural diseases that occur, and pesticides can make our food disease-free. Obviously, the pesticides must be used wisely. But this points to an important issue: Natural is not necessarily better. Nature is not good; in fact, nature can be quite maleficent. After all, diseases are natural; curing disease is the most unnatural thing in the world.

On the eighth day after my grandson's birth, we celebrated his *brit milah*—ritual circumcision. We did not do it for health reasons, although I believe there are health benefits to being circumcised. Rather, we did it for religious reasons. It is probably the oldest tradition in Judaism, leading back to Abraham circumcising himself and his son Isaac in the Bible. The Torah never gives the reason why it takes place on the eighth day. But I believe there is a powerful message related to this idea of moving beyond nature.

Seven days symbolizes the completion of nature. God created the world in six days and rested on the seventh. Seven has always been a sign of completeness in Judaism. So we wait until seven days have passed, but on the eighth day we make a mark in the flesh. The message is that the world of nature is incomplete. Our job is to complete God's work. Throughout this book we have shown how nature is in process, that nature is somehow incomplete. Our job is to be God's partners to complete nature.

The reason Jews do not worship nature is that nature is incomplete. As we mentioned in the chapter on ethics, in Judaism there is no tradition of natural law, so important in Catholic theology. We do not teach the doctrine that we can learn right and wrong from nature. So too, in the story at the beginning of this chapter about the frog and the scorpion, because something is in someone's nature does not make it right. We humans have many natural tendencies, whether for greed, for anger, or for sexual promiscuity, but because these are natural does not make them right. Monogamy is not natural, and yet the Torah sees it as the ideal way to live. Our goal is to move beyond our nature. Or perhaps a better way to put it, our job is perfect nature, both within ourselves and within the world.

The midrash contains a wonderful passage:

> A king had two servants he truly loved, and he wanted to test them to see who was worthier. He gave each one a measure of wheat and a measure of linen. One servant carefully guarded the wheat and the linen, making no changes. The other took the wheat, ground it into flour, and baked a delicious cake. He took the linen, weaved it, and created a beautiful placemat. When the king asked to see what the two servants had done, the foolish one brought out the untouched wheat and linen. The wise one

brought out the cake sitting on the placemat. It is clear which servant the king chose as the worthier.[9]

The prayerbook brings a wonderful interpretation of this midrash:

> When creating the world, God deliberately made everything a bit incomplete. Instead of making bread grow out of the earth, God made wheat grow, so that we might bake it into bread. Instead of making the earth of bricks, God make it of clay, so that we might bake the clay into bricks. Why? So that we could become God's partners in Creation.[10]

We can appreciate nature as God's creation. Nature can inspire us. But we ought not to worship nature. Nature is incomplete and our job is to complete it. This idea will become even more clear when we study Lurianic kabbalah in the chapter on mysticism. First, we must turn to study of light in a chapter that truly studies modern science.

---

9. *Midrash Eliyahu Zuta*, chapter 2.
10. *Siddur Hadash*, 80.

CHAPTER 10

Light—If Light Is a Wave, What Is Waving?

Arthur Eddington (1882–1944) was one of the most important astrophysicists of the twentieth century. He is perhaps most famous for testing Einstein's theory of general relativity and declaring to the world that it is true. In 1919 during a full eclipse of the sun, Eddington measured the location of certain stars, usually hidden by bright sunlight. Einstein had claimed that the mass of the sun was sufficient to distort space and cause the light to bend. Eddington took careful pictures, measured the position of the stars, and declared that Einstein was right. The sun's gravity was causing the starlight to bend. This was the moment that Einstein became famous.

There is an apocryphal story that after these events, a woman approached Eddington and said to him, "I understand you are one of only three people in the world who understand Einstein's theory." Eddington thought about it for a second, and then responded, "Who is the third?"

As part of my graduate studies I challenged myself with a class in the theory of relativity. It was an independent study conducted by a physics professor. I learned a good deal, but my biggest memory of the class is the professor asking before every problem, "Who is the observer?" Space and time depend on the observer. Changing observers will change the result of a problem.

For example, one problem that we worked on was a train a quarter mile long passing through a tunnel a quarter mile long. Suppose the train was moving at more than half the speed of light, a very fast train. Someone standing near the tunnel would see a much shorter train. One could easily put a gate at each end of the tunnel and trap the train inside for a moment. Someone standing in the train would see a much shorter tunnel. The train would be longer than the tunnel and could not be trapped inside by gates. How could that be?

The answer depends on the observer. Someone by the tunnel would see the gates close at the same time. Someone on the train would see the gates close at different times, not trapping the train. Different observers see events at different times. But it took me hours of work with the professor to get my mind around this seeming paradox.

What Is Light?[1]

On the first day God created light. But the Bible is not clear about the source of this light. There was still no sun, no moon, no stars, nothing to give off light. So what was this primordial light? The Talmud seeks to answer that question:

> Rabbi Elazar said, the light created by the blessed Holy One on the first day, Adam could gaze at it and see from one end of the universe to the other. When the Holy One blessed be He foresaw the generation of the Flood and the generation of the Dispersion (the generation of the Tower of Babel) and how their deeds would become corrupt, He immediately hid it from them, as is written, "the light of the wicked is withheld" (Job 38:15). For whom did He hide it? For the righteous in the time to come.[2]

What is light? The answer seems obvious. But trying to pin down the true nature of light will take us to the edge of some of the most fascinating areas of science, from relativity to quantum physics.

"And God said, Let there be light, and there was light." So begins the first act of creation. According to Rabbi Samuel bar Nachman, "God wrapped Himself in a white garment, and the garment illuminated the

---

1. The material at the beginning of this chapter is an expansion of an essay I wrote: Gold, "Let There Be Light."

2. *Babylonian Talmud, Hagigah* 12a.

universe from one end to the other."[3] This image became central to the mystical vision of creation, which we will explore in the next chapter.

Scientists give another explanation. A popular T-shirt reads:

And God said

$$\blacktriangledown \cdot E = 4\pi\rho$$

$$\blacktriangledown \cdot B = 0$$

$$\blacktriangledown \times E = -1/c\, \partial B\, /\, \partial t$$

$$\blacktriangledown \times B = 1/c\, (4\,\pi\, J + \partial E\, /\, \partial t)$$

and there was light.

These are the four elegant equations discovered by the English physicist James Clerk Maxwell (1831–1879) to describe electromagnetism. Light has a scientific explanation, formulated by the brilliant equations of Maxwell and others.

So who is right, the mystics or the scientists? The term *light* may be precise, scientific, objective, to use the phrase of the logical empiricists "verifiable." It may be universal in its understanding. But do we really know what light is? Maxwell's four equations describe how a moving electric charge creates a magnetic field. The equations also describe how a moving magnetic field creates an electric field. Electricity creates magnetism, which then creates electricity, which then creates magnetism, ad infinitum. These alternating fields move forth in the form of a wave, similar to the waves in the ocean. These waves move at a constant speed, the "c" in the equations, approximately 186,000 miles per second in a vacuum.

Visible light is really a wave of electromagnetic radiation. Light is only one small piece of a vast electromagnetic spectrum. Waves come in all sizes, from low-energy, long wavelength to high-energy, tiny wavelength. The lower-energy waves of electromagnetic radiation are radio waves. When we listen to the ball game as we drive in our car, we are merely using technology to capture these low-energy waves. Moving up the energy band, we find microwaves, which we can use to make popcorn, then infrared radiation, which are given off when objects are heated. Then we reach the small tiny spectrum of visible light, from lower-energy red through yellow, green, blue, and higher-energy violet. Visible light varies from 7500 angstroms for red light to about 3800 angstroms for violet light. (An angstrom is a unit of length equal to 10–8 cm.)

As tiny as these wavelengths are, the universe produces even higher-energy, shorter wavelength electromagnetic radiation. These are ultraviolet

3. *Genesis Rabbah* 3.1.

rays, which can damage our skin if we do not wear sunscreen. Then come X-rays, which have the potential to cause great damage. That is why the X-ray technician leaves the room to take the X-ray, and we wear a lead covering for the part of the body not being X-rayed. Finally, there are gamma rays, whose wavelength approaches those of atoms. These are produced in huge quantities by the nuclear fusion at the heart of the sun. Fortunately, they lose much of their energy traveling to the surface of the sun, so that we are not bathed in gamma rays. Such radiation exposure would be extremely damaging.

All of these are really the same phenomenon, oscillating fields of electricity and magnetism heading through the universe at a constant speed c. What is the light God created on the first day? He created electromagnetic waves. Nonetheless, this opens the door to many profound problems. When we think about a wave, something must be waving. In the oceans, the water waves. When we hear sounds, the air is waving. (We cannot hear sounds in a vacuum.) When we are at a football game and someone starts a wave, the fans are waving. You cannot start a wave in an empty stadium. What is waving when light passes by?

Scientists once believed that there was an invisible substance called the luminiferous ether, sometimes simply called ether, through which light waves propagated. Ether filled the universe and light waves were simply a disturbance of the ether. Then Albert Michaelson and E. W. Morley designed an experiment in 1887 to try to detect the ether. They believed the speed of light ought to vary depending on which way the earth is moving through the ether. To their surprise, they discovered that the speed of light was constant, no matter which way they measured it. The obvious but surprising conclusion is that there is no ether. Electromagnetic waves move at a constant speed no matter how it is measured. This disturbing fact led to Albert Einstein (1879–1955) and a revolution in how we view the universe.

Relativity

The year 1905 is known in the annals of science as *Annus Mirabilis*—"the miraculous year." During that year Einstein, a young clerk in the patent office in Bern, Switzerland, published four groundbreaking scientific papers. With those papers Einstein revolutionized how we see the universe. One of those papers was titled "On the Electrodynamics of Moving Bodies." With that simple-sounding title, Einstein established his theory of special relativity.

Einstein began with a thought experiment. What would happen if a human being sped up next to a wave of light? Would the light appear to slow down? After all, if our car speeds up next to a moving train, the train appears to slow down in relation to our car. If we are moving at the same speed as the train, it might appear that the train is standing still. Light ought to behave the same way. So too, Einstein wondered what would happen if he watched a distant clock tower while traveling away from the tower at the speed of light. New light from the clock would never reach him, and it would appear as if the clock stopped, and time stood still. Would the same happen if he could catch up to that ray of light? Would time stand still?

Einstein's thought experiments led to a radical rethinking of the nature of the universe. According to Einstein, the speed of light must remain constant no matter how fast we move. This is actually the result of the principle of relativity, a principle that goes back to Galileo. It says that the laws of physics are the same in all frames of reference moving at a constant speed. A ball would behave the same way whether we are bouncing on the ground or bouncing it in a jet plane moving 600 miles per hour. So too, based on Maxwell's equations, the speed of light is always c, even if we are moving at half the speed of c.

How is this possible? Here Einstein built on the earlier work of Hendrik Lorentz (1853–1928). Lorentz had worked out the mathematics for the transformation of space and time, so that the speed of light would remain constant. For Lorentz this was a mathematical device that had nothing to do with reality. Einstein's radical idea is that space and time really do change depending on the frame of reference of the observer. Someone who watches another frame of reference move past them at a very fast speed will see space shrink in the direction of motion and will see time slow down on that frame of references. But the speed of light will always remain the same. Space and time are not absolutes built into the universe. They are dependent on the observer. The roots of this idea were taught by Immanuel Kant when he spoke of categories of the mind, and how it organizes what it sees in the universe. To Kant, space and time were categories in our minds rather than out there in the real world.

In a similar way, simultaneity has disappeared under Einstein. Two events might occur at the same time for one observer and at separate times for another observer. Imagine someone in the middle of a train shining a light. The light will hit the front and the back of the train at the same time. Now, imagine someone in the station watching the train go by very fast. The front of the train has moved further away from the shining of the light, while the back of the train has moved closer. But the speed of light is always constant. The light will hit the back of the train before the front of the train. Space, time, and simultaneity depend on the observer.

The results of this changing of space and time can be strange indeed. For example, let us suppose that there are two twins, one who stays on earth and one who takes off in a very fast spaceship for a period of time. When the traveling twin returns, he will discover that he is much younger than his brother who stayed home. If he traveled fast enough, it is possible that he hardly aged at all while his brother has become an old man. Experiments have demonstrated that special relativity is absolutely true.

One can further ask, what about the mass of an object? What would happen if I added energy to an object, causing it to accelerate toward the speed of light? According to Einstein, the faster the object goes, the greater its mass would be. To reach the speed of light would require infinite mass, obviously impossible. Here Einstein wrote a second paper that same year, claiming that energy is mass and mass is energy. Adding energy adds to the mass. The formula Einstein taught is probably the most famous in physics: $E=mc^2$ or the energy is the mass times the speed of light squared. Out of this formula the United States harnessed this energy and developed the atomic bomb, which ended World War II.

Einstein called this the special theory of relativity because it deals with a special case, measuring light in a reference frame traveling in uniform motion. Einstein next asked, what would happen to light in a reference frame not traveling in uniform motion? What if the reference frame were accelerating? For example, imagine you are in a box in free fall toward the earth. You are doing physics experiments (and ignoring what will happen when you hit the ground). Galileo had long ago proven that every object in the box, no matter what the weight, would fall at the same rate. What if someone shines a light in the box? Would the light fall to earth? Einstein theorized that gravity would affect light just as it affects matter.

Einstein came up with what is known as the theory of equivalence. There is no difference between a box falling to earth under gravity and a box accelerating into space by a rocket. In an accelerating box if you shine a light, assuming you are accelerating fast enough, the light will appear to move downward on the opposite wall. After all, the box has moved upward during the time it took for the light to shine across the rocket. So the light in the falling box would bend downward toward the earth. But how is that possible?; light always travels in a straight line. Here was Einstein's great insight. Gravity actually distorts space and time, so that a straight line would bend. To summarize, matter causes space and time to curve, and that curvature affects how matter and light move through space and time.

Einstein called this the general law of relativity. The mathematics are complicated, involving a mathematical concept know as tensors. Walter Isaacson, in his best-selling biography of Einstein, called a tensor "a vector on steroids." Einstein actually turned to his friend mathematician Marcel Grossmann (1878–1936), who taught Einstein tensor theory and non-Euclidean geometry, allowing him to build the theory. But the basic idea is simple: gravity bends space and time so that light is affected by gravity.

Einstein's work was only theoretical and still needed to be proven. In 1919 a British scientist named Arthur Eddington (mentioned in the story at the beginning of this chapter) traveled to the island of Príncipe off the coast of Africa to photograph a solar eclipse. During the eclipse, with the moon blocking the sun, nearby stars became visible. As Einstein predicted, the stars appeared slightly out of place, their light bent by the gravity of the sun. Eddington's confirmation of Einstein's work made Einstein famous, and changed forever how we view light. By the way, Eddington was not only a great scientist but a strong believer in panpsychism, the theory that mind permeates matter. We explored this theory in our chapter on evolution.

Our exploration of light will turn even stranger. We will look at a third paper Einstein published in that miraculous year, the one on the photoelectric effect. He actually won his Nobel Prize for this paper rather than relativity. (His fourth paper was on Brownian motion, helping to establish that atoms really exist.) But to look at the photoelectric effect, we need to turn to the other great revolution in physics—quantum theory.

Quantum Theory

Before Einstein began to think about the photoelectric effect, the physicist Max Planck was already speculating about something called black body radiation. If electromagnetism is a wave, then when a black body is heated up it should give off radiation at all energy levels. But the energy seems to only be given off at discreet levels. Planck theorized the existence of a constant number, today known as Planck's constant, which causes the discreet, one might say graininess, of how energy is given off by a black body.

Einstein built on Planck's idea. He theorized that light can only be given off at discreet energy levels, and therefore light was more like a particle than a wave. He called these particles of light photons. Electrons absorb electromagnetic energy in discreet numbers and also give off energy in discreet numbers. Niels Bohr (1885–1962), one of the great founders of quantum theory, used this idea to explain the Bohr atom. Atoms absorb certain energy levels or frequencies of light, allowing electrons to jump from one orbit to the next orbit. This is what came to be known as the quantum leap, not a huge leap but the smallest possible for an electron. When the electron falls to a lower orbit, it gives off energy at precise levels. This explained a phenomenon that had long puzzled physicists, why different elements give off radiation in distinct colors. A particular color of light represents a particular energy level. This also explains why the electron does not give off all its energy and spin into the nucleus. An electron can only give off energy at discreet levels.

The strangeness is only beginning. Einstein discovered that light is not just a wave but a particle. Another founder of quantum theory, Louis de Broglie (1892–1987), taught that electrons are not only particles but waves. On the tiniest level of the universe, everything has a particle-like nature and a wave-like nature. Other great thinkers would build on this strangeness. Werner Heisenberg (1901–1976) would discover the uncertainty principle, that it is impossible to know with certainty both the location and the momentum of a particle. It is not simply that we cannot measure the location and momentum, no exact location and momentum exists.

Erwin Schrodinger (1887–1961) developed a formula for calculating the behavior of any quantum system. Every quantum system is a superposition of all possible states. Schrodinger's equation is the sum of all those states with a coefficient showing the odds that any particular state will turn up.[4] Only the act of observation causes the sum to collapse and one particular state of being to show up. (This is often called the Copenhagen interpretation of quantum mechanics. There are other interpretations.) Schrodinger would also introduce his famous cat, both alive and dead at the same time, until one looks inside a box, causing the Schrodinger equation to collapse. Quantum theory is one of the most successful in the history of science, and also one of the strangest. That is why the great physicist Richard Feynman (1918–1988) famously said, "Anyone who says they understand quantum mechanics does not understand quantum mechanics."

Let us return to our discussion of light. Is it a wave or is it a particle? The answer is both—and neither. It depends on how the experiment is done. In some experiments light behaves like a wave and in some experiments light behaves like a particle. Make two openings in a wall and shine a light through it and it creates an interference pattern like a wave. Put a Geiger counter–type device at one of the openings to tell where the light passed through and the interference pattern disappears; the Geiger counter clicks

---

4. Actually, the coefficient is a complex number. Multiply it by its complex conjugate and you get a real number between 0 and 1, giving the odds that this state will appear. Only when an observer measures that state does the formula collapse, one coefficient becoming 1 and the others 0. Only observation creates a reality we can know.

as if light is a particle. It is as if the very act of observing changes the nature of light from a wave to a particle.

Maybe there is a way to determine the essence of light. If we were able to invent a very powerful microscope that could make a photon of light visible to the naked eye, we might find a definition. But according to quantum theory this is impossible. The very act of looking at the photon changes it. According to the Heisenberg uncertainty principle, if we measured the momentum it would change the location and if we measured the location we would change the momentum. We cannot pin light down. In fact, we cannot pin anything down; the very act of observing something changes it.

This brings is to an argument we discussed in the introduction to this book. Does science tell us what is really out there? Or does science simply measure what our mind can know, without making a claim about reality? Does science give us real knowledge or simply epistemic knowledge? Einstein insisted that we can know reality. Bohr insisted that we cannot know reality, only the results of our experiments. Bohr and Einstein would participate in a series of very public debates on the nature of reality, with Bohr insisting that reality is totally probabilistic and Einstein replying that "God does not play dice with the universe."

The one clear result of this entire debate is the role of consciousness in quantum theory. When no observer looks at light it is a wave. When a conscious observer looks at light it becomes a particle. Consciousness is a fundamental part of the universe. To pin down the importance of consciousness, let us explore one more aspect of quantum theory, known as entanglement. Two particles light years apart can become entangled, so that despite the distance what happens to one instantaneously affects the other.

Entanglement

We have mentioned that according to quantum theory, or at least the Copenhagen interpretation of quantum theory, reality consists of a superposition of possibilities. Only when an observer measures that reality does the Schrodinger equation collapse, and one possibility becomes that reality. Observation creates reality. Until then, reality is just a series of probabilities.

Einstein hated this idea that reality is simply probabilities, that God plays dice with the universe. In 1935 Einstein together with two younger colleagues, Boris Podolsky and Nathan Rosen, came up with their greatest challenge to quantum physics, known as the EPR paradox, named using the first letter of the three authors' last names. The paradox challenged the probability basis of quantum theory, trying to prove that there was some underlying reality that behaved according to classical mechanics. Einstein called this underlying reality "hidden variables." Supposedly Bohr was so shocked when he read the EPR paradox that he could not sleep until he found a way to prove Einstein wrong.

To give an example of the EPR paradox, suppose a particle of zero spin breaks apart, sending two particles in opposite directions. According to quantum theory, each of those particles is a superposition of two possibilities, spin up and spin down. They travel separately until they are a light year apart. Then someone observes and measures one of the particles. Suppose she measures it as spin up. Since spin is a conserved quality, the other particle instantly becomes spin down. But they were a light year apart with no way to communicate with one another. How did the second particle know that someone measured the first? Einstein said that there must be some hidden variable already present in the particles when they broke apart. Without that, the universe would permit what Einstein called "spooky action at a distance."

Was Einstein correct? Are there hidden variables? Irish physicist John Stewart Bell (1928–1990) came up with an important mathematical theorem, basically an inequality that would hold true only if quantum mechanics is correct, if there is spooky action at a distance. Bell's inequality has been tested in the laboratory numerous times and the results are clear. Einstein was wrong. Particles can instantly affect one another even when separated by a great distance. Or to use the language of physics, particles are entangled. It is as if particles can touch each other across vast distances of space.

I am not a physicist, but the EPR paradox and Bell's theorem have fascinated me for years. Allow me to offer my own amateur understanding, which fits in with the idealism of this chapter. Long ago Descartes differentiated between two substances, matter and mind. Matter is *res extensa*, taking up space. Mind is *res cogitans*, pure thought that does not take up space. In space, items could not instantly affect one another if vastly separated. But mind does not take up space. A mind in one place could affect a mind in another place. Minds can touch over a distance. Have you ever thought about someone you have not thought about for a long time, and suddenly they telephone you? Minds touch each other even when separated.

Perhaps entanglement exists because on some fundamental level everything is mind. Minds can touch and affect other minds over a distance. Perhaps physics is catching up to an idea that mystics, both Eastern and Western, have known for centuries. Everything is part of some ultimately reality, and everything touches everything else. And if this is true, perhaps light is simply a metaphor for mind.

Light as Mind

The thirteenth-century mystic Azriel of Gerona wrote:

> Whatever one implants firmly in the mind becomes the essential things. So if you pray and offer a blessing to God, or if you wish your intention to be true, imagine that you are light. All around you—in every corner and on every side—is light. Turn to your right and you will find shining light, to your left, splendor, a radiant light. Between them, up above, the light of the Presence. Surrounding that, the light of life. Above it all, a crown of light—crowning the aspirations of thought, illumining the paths of imagination, spreading the radiance of vision. This light is unfathomable and endless.[5]

Mystics have long seen the collection between mind and light. Matthew T. Kapstein, in his anthology *The Presence of Light*, writes in his own essay:

> Light, under one description or another, is a universal religious symbol if anything is, and most religions make literal or metaphoric reference to experiences of light in various contexts. Nevertheless, it is striking that spiritual techniques focusing upon light became particularly accentuated in a number of particular religious movements, often described as "mystical," in late antiquity and the medieval period.[6]

Already Plato evoked light as a metaphor for mind. Arthur Zajonc, in his book *Catching the Light: The Entwined History of Light and Mind*, writes: "Plato used sight as a metaphor for all knowing, calling the psyche's own organ of perception the 'eye of the soul' or 'the mind's eye.'"[7] In a similar way, Lawrence Wu writes: "Philosophers have long been using the metaphors 'light' and 'mirror' to represent the nature of mind and its functionings because of their richness of meanings."[8] Although Wu does not discuss Jewish mysticism in particular, he does discuss Plotinus, who we explored in chapter 8. Wu writes: "Plotinus's theory of continuing creation as emanation seems to be based on the metaphor of light. This conception of the Universal

---

5. Quoted by Matt, *Essential Kabbalah*, 110.
6. Kapstein, *Presence of Light*, 285.
7. Zajonc, *Catching the Light*, 22.
8. Wu, "Light and Mirror," 145.

Mind, the One and the Good as an overflowing fountain of light attests to this claim."[9]

How did the mystics look at this light? The light according to the *Zohar* is not part of the creation. God did not create light out of nothing as the beginning of Genesis seems to indicate. Rather, the light was always there; the light always existed. Alluding to an ancient midrashic tradition,[10] the *Zohar* states[11]: "Let there be light." Light that already existed. This light is a hidden mystery." If you take light to mean mind, then mind always existed. The creation story is one of mind flowing into the world. With this presumption that light means mind, we are ready to turn to Jewish mysticism, and in particular, the creation story in the classic book of Jewish mysticism, the *Zohar*.

9. Wu, "Light and Mirror," 151.

10. *Genesis Rabbah* 3:2.

11. *Zohar*, I 16b.

CHAPTER 11

Mysticism—Can Our Souls Touch God?

Our rabbis taught, Four men entered the Garden [in Hebrew Pardes or paradise],
Ben Azzai, Ben Zoma, Aher [Elishah ben Abulia], and R. Akiba. R. Akiba said,
"when you arrive at the stones of pure marble, say not 'water, water.'" Ben Azzai
looked and died. Ben Zoma looked and became demented. Aher cut the shoots
[became a heretic.] Only R. Akiba departed unhurt.[1]

There is a wedding tradition I find very meaningful. At a Jewish wedding, after the bride and groom walk down the aisle and before the ceremony begins, the bride walks around the groom. Traditionally she walks around seven times, for the seven days of creation. Some brides walk around three times, corresponding to the three times Hosea uses the word "betroth": "I will betroth you forever, I will betroth you in righteousness and in justice, in kindness and in mercy, I will betroth you in faithfulness and you shall know the Lord" (Hosea 2:21–22). The tradition has roots in kabbalah or Jewish mysticism.

Whenever people study kabbalah, I warn them that Jewish mysticism is not egalitarian. Masculine and feminine have different roles. In kabbalah the feminine aspects of God are the protective aspects, forming a fence, like the protective wall of the cell. The symbolism of this ancient custom is that the bride becomes the protective fence of the household.

---

1. *Babylonia Talmud, Hagigah* 14b.

Occasionally, I have a couple who want to keep the tradition, but in a more egalitarian way. The bride will walk around the groom three times, the groom will walk around the bride three times, and then they will walk around each other, a kind of do-si-do. I will allow it, but I will first attempt to convince them to observe the traditional way. Something valuable is lost in the mystical message when we remove gender differentiation. To the mystics, gender was essential to understanding God.

What Is Mysticism?

Most faiths have a tradition of mysticism. Mysticism is based on the idea that there is an ultimate reality that is unified and accessible to human beings. The goal is for individual selves, through various spiritual practices, to unite with that ultimate reality. Such spiritual practices as fasting, chanting, meditation, and yoga can help the individual lose that sense of self and connect with that ultimate spiritual reality. Most mystical traditions also include theosophy, or an understanding of the inner workings of this spiritual reality or of God. That will be the focus of this chapter, as we explore the inner life of God in both the *Zohar* and Lurianic kabbalah.

Mysticism has a long history among such Eastern religious traditions as Hinduism and Buddhism. These traditions are not built around the personhood of God like religions in the West. They are much more likely to speak about an ultimate reality, called by Hindus *Brahman*. Buddhists also reject the notion of an individual soul or self. Each human is part of that ultimate reality. It becomes a natural part of these religious traditions to lose the self to the ultimate reality, much as an individual wave is part of the greater ocean. (This metaphor is often used to describe mystical experiences.) Meditation then becomes a way for the self to connect with something greater.

Mysticism is a bit more difficult to understand in Western traditions where there is a belief in a personal God beyond creation. If God is transcendent, how can individuals achieve unity with that God? Western mystical traditions often find their root in ancient mystery religions and practices. But it was the pagan interpreter of Plato named Plotinus (204/5–270 CE), discussed in the chapter on idealism, who laid out an image of reality that influenced Jewish, Christian, and Muslim mysticism. Plotinus imagined an ultimate reality flowing through a series of steps, ultimately ending in the physical world. We used the metaphor of a multilevel punch bowl with the punch flowing down from higher to lower levels. The lowest level is the material world, which is farthest from the source. But the individual soul, by certain spiritual practices, can climb up to higher levels.

In Judaism, there is a long mystical tradition known as *kabbalah* from a Hebrew root meaning "to receive." It is built on the idea of emanation or a flow from the Godhead. The source of the flow is known as *Ein Sof* ("infinity" or "without end") and the flow goes through a series of emanations known as *sefirot*. These emanations are often drawn like limbs on a body. The most important book of Jewish mystical speculation appeared in thirteenth-century Spain and is known as the *Zohar*. Although Orthodox Jews attribute the *Zohar* to the second-century Talmudic rabbi Shimon bar Yochai, most scholars believe it was written in Spain by the mystic Moshe de Leon (1250–1305). Later a Jewish mystic named Isaac Luria (1534–1572), who lived in Safed in what is today Israel, developed a new mystical system expanding on these ideas.

Kabbalah (or as Christians call it, cabbala) influenced Christianity. Such Renaissance philosophers as Giordano Bruno (1548–1600) studied cabbala before writing his own speculations about the nature of the universe. Bruno was burnt at the stake by the Catholic Church for his ideas, including an infinite universe. Nonetheless, Christianity developed a long mystical tradition of its own. This is often built on contemplation of the Christ, and is based on the notion that there are spiritual truths that cannot be achieved through the intellect but only through such contemplation. Christians often attribute the beginning of Christian mysticism to the sixth-century writer Dionysius the Areopagite, also known as pseudo-Dionysius. Influenced by Plotinus, he used the metaphor of a sculptor cutting away material to achieve a work of art; so the mystic must chip away at extraneous matter to achieve oneness with Christ.

There have been numerous Christian mystics. This includes both men and women, such as Teresa of Avila, Hildegard of Bingen, and John of the Cross. Perhaps the most famous Christian mystic is Meister Eckhart (1260–1328), who taught that there is a true Godhead beyond God that cannot be known rationally, but only through immediate experience. This Godhead can be reached through detachment from this world (teachings very similar to Buddhism). Eckhart remains influential among Christian mystics today.

Islam also has a long mystic tradition known as Sufism. Most Sufi orders trace their traditions to Mohammed's son-in-law Ali ibn Abi Talib (601?–661). Sufism emphasizes that knowledge comes through working with a teacher rather than learning from books. Again, there is an emphasis on removing one's self from the world to connect to a greater reality.

Today, there is a growth of interest in mysticism as well as various esoteric traditions. Many in the West, raised in the classic Abrahamic faiths, have turned to Buddhism and other Eastern traditions in order to connect to ultimate reality. Others are exploring kabbalah, Sufism, or the writings of such Christians as Meister Eckhart. Perhaps in reaction to the scientific viewpoint that everything is material, mystics seek to find the reality beyond the material.

Judaism recognizes that there is a danger in mystical speculation, best associated with the legend of the four rabbis entering the *pardes* quoted at the beginning of this chapter. The term *pardes* means "orchard" or "paradise," but it also stands for the four ways of interpreting the Torah. One can use *p'shat*—"the plain meaning," *remez*—"allegory," *drash*—"interpretation," and *sod*—literally "secret, mystical interpretation." The four rabbis were involved in such mystical interpretation. It is noteworthy that Rabbi Akiba would say, "when you arrive at the stones of pure marble, say not 'water, water.'" In one of our interpretations of the creation story, when we speak of the spirit of God hovering over the water, that water stands for matter. Rabbi Akiba warns that the mystic should not mistake what he sees for physical matter, but rather something spiritual, something beyond water.

The Mishnah warns about mystical speculation:

> Do not teach about the works of creation with two people. Do not teach about the works of the chariot [the vision of the chariot in the first chapter of Ezekiel] with one person unless they are wise in understanding and knowledge. Anyone who looks at four things, it would be better if he never came into the world. What is above. What is below. What is before. What is after.[2]

In this chapter we are going to ignore the Mishnah's warnings and speculate on the works of creation. We will explore the creation story in the *Zohar*.[3] Then we will explore how the great mystic Isaac Luria reinterpreted that story to build one of the most influential mythical visions in Judaism. Using the traditions of Jewish mysticism, we will tell a creation story.

2. *Misnhah, Hagigah* 2:1.

3. Much of the material in this section comes from Gold, "Whiteheadian."

The *Sefirot*

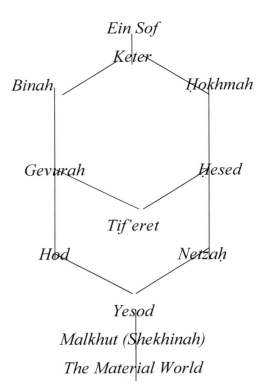

Ein Sof, Ayin, and Keter

Our creation story begins with the unknown and unknowable. *Ein Sof* literally means "without end." Mathematicians in Israel use this Hebrew phrase to refer to infinity. To quote the *Zohar*:

> He (Rabbi Shimon) said, We have already taught that it (the inability to know) extends to *Ein Sof* for all attachment, unification, and completion is to be hidden in that hidden place which is not perceived or known, and which contains the will of all wills. *Ein Sof* cannot be known, and does not produce end nor beginning like the primal *ayin* (nothing), which does bring forth beginning and end. What is beginning? The supernal point which is the beginning of all, concealed and resting within thought, and producing end that is called "The end of the matter'" (Ecclesiastes 12:13). But there are no ends, no wills, no lights, no sparks in *Ein Sof*. All these sparks and lights depend on it for their existence, but they are not in a position to perceive. That which knows, but does not know, is none but the Supernal Will, the secret of all secrets, *ayin*.[4]

One notes from this quote that the *Zohar* also uses the phrase *ayin*— "nothing." The *Ein Sof* is nothing in that we can know nothing about it. But this also allows us to use the classical Jewish phrase creation from nothing, *yesh m'ayin*—"something from nothing." The *Ein Sof* may be nothing but it is filled with potential. This is similar to the way quantum physicists teach that a vacuum is not really a vacuum at all but filled with quantum potential and virtual particles that come and go out of existence. Let us look at how Daniel Matt, who recently finished a scholarly translation of the *Zohar*, describes this vacuum:

> For the kabbalists, there *is* a "'something" that emerges from "nothing," but the nothing is brimming with overwhelming divine reality; it is *mahut*, the "whatness," the quiddity of God. The something is not a physical object but rather the first ray of divine wisdom, which, as Job indicates [see Job 28:12 which can be translated "But wisdom from nothing is it found, where is the place of understanding"], emerges from *ayin*. It is the primordial point that marks the beginning of the unfolding of God.[5]

Within *Ein Sof* there is a desire, a supernal will, to manifest itself in the world. We have already mentioned that this is where Jewish mysticism

4. *Zohar* II 239a.
5. Matt, "*Ayin*," 78.

breaks with classic Neoplatonism. In Neoplatonism the emanation is like a brook flowing from a spring; the spring has no desire to create the brook. Whenever Jewish thinkers interpreted Plotinus, they added another layer of being, a primal desire or will. This primordial desire becomes the first of the ten *sefirot*, known as *Keter*. *Keter* literally means "crown" but comes to signify this primordial desire. Some argue that *Keter* is simply another name for *Ein Sof,* others that *Keter* is separate from *Ein Sof,* the highest of the ten *sefirot*. With *Keter* the emanation begins.

How did this early emanation take place? Let us turn to the *Zohar* itself:

> At the head of potency of the King, He engraved engravings in luster on high. A spark of impenetrable darkness flashed within the concealed of the concealed from the head of Infinity—a cluster of vapor forming in formlessness, thrust in a ring, not white, not black, not red, not green, no color at all. As a cord surveyed, it yielded radiant colors. Deep within the spark gushed a flow, splaying colors below, concealed within the concealed of the mystery of *Ein Sof.* It split and did not split its aura, was not known at all, until under the impact of splitting, a single concealed, supernal point shone. Beyond that point nothing is known, so it called *Reshit*, Beginning, first command of all.[6]

Emanation began with an explosion of light; it sounds a good deal like the big bang. The beginning of everything was a bursting of light or energy into the universe.

We have suggested that "light" is really a metaphor for mind. This raises some difficult and profound questions. What does it mean for mind to emanate into the universe? Do parts of mind become separated from other parts of mind? If we say they are separate, do such minds occupy space? Does the primordial mind include these various separate pieces of mind? As mentioned in our chapter on idealism, Alfred North Whitehead sees a world made up of actual entities, bits of consciousness (mind) that appear momentarily and pass out of existence. Whitehead never described where his actual entities came from. This image of separate entities or occasions of experience seems very close to the image of mind emanating into space and time and separating into bits of consciousness. It suggests the image of one consciousness becoming many.

We now turn to the radical reading of the beginning of Genesis mentioned in the beginning of Part III of this book. The first term, *bereishit*, means "with beginning," but rabbinic tradition also translates this term as

6. *Zohar* I 15a.

Ḥokhmah—"wisdom." The *Zohar* translates the first word of the Torah as "with wisdom." *Bara* means "created." *Elohim* means God. But this term, following the term *bara*, is read literally in order. "With wisdom _____ created God." *Elohim* "God" is not the subject doing the creating. Rather, *Elohim* is the object being created. God is not the creator but rather the creation. The subject of the sentence is left blank. Who is doing the creating? Something unmentioned and unknown: *Ein Sof*, *ayin*, or perhaps *Keter*. God is the creation, or to follow our interpretation, mind is the creation. The blank line represents an unknown.

According to this interpretation, God is the universe. And if God means primordial mind, then mind is the universe. This is what we earlier called panentheism; God is both beyond and within creation. It is an idealistic view of reality, everything is mind. Let us continue the story with the various *sefirot* that flow from this initial creation.

Ḥokhmah and Binah

The first level of divine thought is known as *Ḥokhmah* ("wisdom"). *Ḥokhmah* is compared to a first drop of thought, like a point unseparated and undifferentiated. It is the first spark of light. Everything that is needed for the creation of the entire universe is contained in *Ḥokhmah*, as pure potential. Early mystical thinkers saw it much like a sperm or male seed, with the potential to impregnate a female. This image of *Ḥokhmah* is definitely masculine. The idea of gender in relation to the *sefirot* will become extremely important as we work our way down through the *sefirot*.

> A male needs a female to create new life. The feminine *sefirah* corresponding to *Ḥokhmah* is *Binah* ("understanding"). *Binah* is the womb in which the seed of *Ḥokhmah* will be implanted. The *Zohar* will present an image of the seed of *Ḥokhmah* impregnating *Binah*: Radiance! Concealed of concealed struck its aura, which touched and did not touch this point. Then this beginning (the point of *Ḥokhmah*) expanded, building itself a palace worthy of glorious praise. There it sowed seed to give birth, availing worlds.[7]

The seed is *Ḥokhmah*, the palace is *Binah*. Here we see the narrative of the first three *sefirot*. *Keter* is the divine will or desire that grows within *Ein Sof* or the Godhead. *Keter* produces a divine spark that contains all potentials, known as *Ḥokhmah*. *Ḥokhmah* impregnates *Binah*, the divine palace

---

7. *Zohar* I 15a.

or the divine womb. Male and female come together to create a world. At this point the male and female are still not separated: "There was still no separation, male and female as one."[8]

How does separation enter the world? The phrase *tohu vavohu* (Genesis 1:2) is usually translated "unformed and void," the watery chaos that preceded the creation of the world. Nevertheless, the *Zohar* presents a radically different understanding of these two terms. *Tohu* and *bohu* are not formlessness and void. Instead, *tohu* is the primordial matter (*hyle*) and *bohu* is the primordial form. Creation is about bringing matter and form together, taking *tohu* and turning it into *bohu*. The *Zohar* teaches:

> *Tohu*—a colorless, formless realm, not embraced by the mystery of form. Now within form—as one contemplates it, not form at all. Everything has a garment in which to be clothed, except for this: though appearing upon it, it does not exist at all, never did. *Bohu*—this has shape and form; stones sunk within the shell of *tohu*, emerging from the shell in which they are sunk, conveying benefit to the world. Through the form of a garment they convey benefit from above to below, ascending from below to above.[9]

Matt comments on this: "Once the forms of *bohu* emerge from the *tohu*, they clothe matter and enable the things of the world to exist. They transmit the stream of emanation from the *sefirot* above to the world below."[10] Here, we see the first hints of how matter comes about in a world of emanation. The emanation takes the primordial formless matter and gives it form.

As form takes on matter, separation enters the world. And with separation sadness enters the world. Rabbinic tradition speaks of how, on the second day of creation, the Torah never says, "God saw that it was good." The reason is because on the second day, God separated the upper and the lower waters. In fact, the midrash teaches how the waters cried out for each other.[11] This idea of separation leading to sadness is a major theme in the *Zohar*. One difference is that the Hebrew Bible speaks of the separation as occurring between the upper and lower waters, the *Zohar* turns this separation on its side. It becomes a separation between right and left. In the next section we will develop the *sefirot* on the right representing the masculine aspects of reality and the *sefirot* on the left representing the feminine aspects of reality. Thus, in the *Zohar*, the separation is not simply between the various *sefirot*, but also between the masculine and feminine.

8. *Zohar* I 15b.
9. *Zohar* I 16a.
10. Matt, *Zohar*, I 120.
11. *Genesis Rabbah* 13:13.

The Next Six Sefirot

The first of these next six *sefirot* is *Ḥesed*, often translated as "lovingkind-ness." The term has multiple meanings in Hebrew, which vary from "love" to "mercy." It implies reaching out one's hand to another. *Ḥesed* is identified with the first of the patriarchs, Abraham, known for his overwhelming kind-ness and hospitality. In kabbalistic thought, *Ḥesed* is considered a masculine trait, on the right side of the symbolic tree of *sefirot*. *Ḥesed* is marked by outreach and benevolence and by a desire to give to others. As important as *Ḥesed* is, a world built simply on *Ḥesed* could not survive. Imagine a home in which the father so desires to practice charity that he gives almost every-thing away. The family would ultimately perish. Now, imagine a biological cell with no protective wall, ready to share all of its nutrients with other cells. It would not survive. Thus, there must be a limit to *Ḥesed* in order for life to sustain itself.

This limit is *Gevurah*, which stands to the left of *Ḥesed*. The word means "strength" in Hebrew, and many kabbalistic texts prefer the word *din*—"judgment." In keeping with our formulation of the *sefirot*, perhaps the term "restraint" offers the best description. *Gevurah* is the feminine trait, much like the mother who keeps her husband from giving everything away. *Gevurah* is the cell membrane that protects the inner contents. Since *Gevurah* is feminine, there is a sense that the female keeps the male from conceding too much, in order to protect the whole. *Gevurah* is the part of reality that is marked by restraint and self-protection. Of course, *Gevurah* also reflects the idea of judgment and severity. *Gevurah* is identified with the second patriarch, Isaac, who lived a far more circumscribed and protected life than either his father or his son. For example, Isaac never set foot out-side the holy land at any time of his life. If *Ḥesed* is responsible for unity or connections within the created world, then *Gevurah* is responsible for the differentiation and uniqueness that marks the created world.

Often *Ḥesed* and *Gevurah* fall out of balance. If there is too much *Ḥesed*, entities will give everything away, thereby losing their integrity and their uniqueness. If there is too much *Gevurah*, entities will retract within themselves and lose all connection to the rest of the world. The proper bal-ance between *Ḥesed* and *Gevurah* is called *Tif'eret*, literally "beauty."

Tif'eret sits at the bottom of a triangle below *Ḥesed* and *Gevurah*. It is identified with Jacob who somehow succeeded in balancing self-absorption with outwardly directed kindness. Implementing *Tif'eret* in the world by seeking balance appears to be the *Zohar's* ideal. *Tif'eret*, meaning balance, comes to represent the masculine aspect of reality, as opposed to *Shekhinah*, which is the feminine aspect of reality.

If we consider this triangle of *sefirot* to be messengers, the next triangle of *sefirot* can be seen as the "sons or messengers" of these three *sefirot*. With these three, we have come a bit closer to the material world in which we live. Perhaps it is easiest to think of *Ḥesed*, *Gevurah*, and *Tif'eret* as referring to emotions or tendencies within the divine self, while the next three *sefirot* (*Netzah*, *Hod*, and *Yesod*) refer to acting out of these emotions or tendencies. Thus, if this lower triangle of *sefirot* refers to action, we are moving closer to the material world, which is a world of physical laws or actions.

Netzah literally means "eternity." If *Ḥesed* is the *desire* to give, then *Netzah* is the *act* of giving. There is a direct line from *Ḥesed* to *Netzah*. *Netzah* is also related to prophecy. According to the *Zohar*, when Jacob was wounded in the thigh while wrestling with the angel,[12] he lost part of his *Netzah*. *Netzah* and *Hod* in balance are the means by which prophecy flows down to the world. When Jacob wrestles with the man, known as the Prince of Esau, *Netzah* is damaged and a part of prophecy is lost. Jacob can only prophesize from his weaker, or left, side. Only with Samuel was full prophecy restored and balance achieved once again.

Parallel to *Ḥesed* and *Netzah*, there is a direct line from *Gevurah* to *Hod*. *Hod* means "glory" or "splendor," and it represents the *act* of protecting, of trying to balance out *Netzah*. The balance point between *Netzah* and *Hod* is called *Yesod* or "foundation." When balance is achieved, the world stands on a solid foundation. But when *Netzah* and *Hod* are off-balance, the world cannot persist. This interpretation fits the common image of the various *sefirot* resting on a human body. *Netzah* rests on the right leg, *Hod* rests on the left leg. In balance, they give a solid foundation, *Yesod*. *Yesod* is also symbolic of the phallus, the masculine drive drawn toward the *Shekhinah*, the feminine drive below.

These six *sefirot* taken together often go by the name *Ti'feret*. They are the masculine aspects of reality. This leads to the tenth *sefirah*, *Malkhut* or *Shekhinah*, the feminine aspects of reality.

Shekhinah

This idea of *Shekhinah* is already developed earlier in the Talmud and midrash. It comes from the Hebrew root *sh-kh-n*, meaning "to dwell." This is God's indwelling in the material world. The rabbis developed the idea that the *Shekhinah* went into exile with the community of Israel. So for example, the Talmud teaches:

---

12. See *Genesis* 32:25–33 for full passage.

Come and see how beloved Israel are to the Holy One, blessed
be He, for wherever they are exiled the *Shekhinah* is with them
. . . and when they are redeemed in the future the *Shekhinah*
will again be with them, as it said, "and the Lord, your God, will
return with your captivity" (Deut. 30:3).[13]

The radical change of the kabbalists was the transformation of *Shekhinah*
from the indwelling of God in the material world to the feminine side of
God.

In the *Zohar*, the *Shekhinah* is the end of the flow of emanation. The
Shekhinah takes a somewhat different role than the other *sefirot*. It is more
passive, absorbing and reflecting higher levels of emanation. On the other
hand, it is the spiritual presence closest to the material world. Arthur Green
writes about this emergence in kabbalistic literature of the *Shekhinah* as the
feminine aspects of God:

A key element in this symbolic universe is the emergence of the
divine female, a figure within the divine-symbolic realm who
serves as consort to the blessed Holy One, God of Israel. The
radical character of this development cannot be overstated. The
singularity and aloneness of God, described almost exclusively
in masculine terms, is the very essence of the monotheistic
revolution wrought by Israel's ancient prophets. It is the God
who by definition has no heavenly consort that seeks out a human beloved in the people Israel, allowing for the essential God-
Israel erotic myth that plays a key role in rabbinic Judaism. Now
Kabbalah comes and tampers with this most essential *datum* of
Jewish devotional life.[14]

Where did the notion of a feminine aspect of God come from? Several
scholars believe that it was a Jewish reaction to the cult of Mary, becoming
extremely popular in the Catholic Church. Whatever the source of the idea,
God now took on explicit masculine and feminine characteristics, which
must be kept in balance.

This brings me to one of the most fascinating insights I learned from
the *Zohar*. Let me begin with a well-known midrash about God shrinking
the moon. In this tale, the sun and the moon were originally equal in size
and stature. However, the moon complained, "How can two kings wear one
crown?" So God responded to the moon, "You are right, shrink yourself."
But then God felt guilty for having shrunk the moon. Therefore, each month
on *Rosh Ḥodesh* or "the new moon," the people Israel must bring a sin

13 *Babylonian Talmud, Megillah* 29a.
14. Green, "Shekhinah," 15–16.

offering for God for the shrinking of the moon. God sinned by making the moon smaller. On *Rosh Hodesh*, the people of Israel atone for God's sin.[15] The book of Isaiah already suggests that someday in the future, the moon and the sun will be equal in stature once again: "The light of the moon shall be like the light of the sun, and the light of the sun shall be sevenfold, like the light of the seven days" (Isaiah 30:26). The first half of the verse suggests that in a Messianic future the moon will once again equal the sun.

The passage quoted above about God shrinking the moon leads to an important theme in the *Zohar*, where the sun and moon take on a deeper meaning. In kabbalistic symbolism, the sun represents the masculine aspects of reality, and the moon represents the feminine aspects of reality. The masculine and feminine principles were originally equal. But, God shrunk the feminine principle and made it secondary to the masculine principle. As the verse in Isaiah quoted about hints, in the future these two principles will become equal once again.

The masculine and the feminine principles are out of balance. There is also a separation between the masculine aspects of reality, symbolized by *Tif'eret*, and the feminine aspects of reality, symbolized by *Shekhinah* or *Malkhut*. But there is also a purpose, a direction, for reality. How can balance be restored? One of the great insights of kabbalah is that human activity has the ability to restore the proper balance between the masculine and feminine aspects of reality. That is the reason why, in the *Siddur* (prayerbook) used by followers of the Jewish mystical tradition, a short meditation appears at the beginning of the morning prayers: "For the purpose of uniting the Holy One, Blessed is He, and the *Shekhinah*." We will develop this idea of the human role in establishing balance further when we look at Lurianic kabbalah.

Lurianic Kabbalah

Isaac Luria, also known as the Holy Ari, built on these ideas in the *Zohar*. He was reacting to a particularly painful time in Jewish history, following the expulsion from Spain, to try to uncover why there is evil in the world. In developing his view of the creation story, he gave Judaism some of its most powerful ideas, including *tzimtzum* (diminishment), *sheverat hakelim* (the breaking of the vessels), *nitzitzot* (holy sparks), and *tikkun* (repair). Luria's story also begins with a primordial light. But in order to make room for that light to emanate into the world, God did an act of self-diminishment called *tzimtzum*. God actually created a space within God's very self to leave room for a universe to grow. In many ways, the Lurianic creation story is far

---

15. *Babylonian Talmud, Hullin* 60b.

more feminine than the biblical creation story. A man creates a child outside himself, spreading his seed into someone else. Creation outside one's self is similar to the beginning of Genesis. On the other hand, a woman creates a child within herself, within a womb, as described by Luria.

God's light burst forth into the empty space, similar to the bursting forth of light described in the *Zohar*. But there were vessels that held those sparks of light. Suddenly, the vessels shattered, causing the sparks of light to spread everywhere. The shattering of the vessels (*sheverat hakelim*) is the cause of the brokenness of the universe. It is intriguing that modern physics speaks of the breaking of symmetry as necessary for the creation of a universe. Are the breaking of the mystical vessels and the breaking of scientific symmetry somehow related? It is a question worth pondering.

The *nitzitzot* or sparks of light scattered everywhere and are now hidden within *kelapot*—coverings or shells. The job of human beings is to uncover those holy sparks and somehow, literally, put God back together again. The term for fixing the world is *tikkun*—"repair" or sometimes *tikkun olam*—"repairing the world." This became one of the most powerful ideas in contemporary Judaism. Many synagogues have a *tikkun* committee. In fact, *Tikkun* is the name of a popular magazine with extremely leftist views. The key idea is that God needs humanity. In Judaism we say the *Sh'ma*: "Hear O Israel the Lord our God, the Lord is One" (Deuteronomy 6:4). But at the end of daily prayers Jews quote the book of Zechariah, "On that day the Lord will be One and His name One" (Zechariah 14:9). God's Oneness is a dream for the future. The role of humanity is to make God one again. Lurianic kabbalah teaches that we humans have the ability and the obligation to repair God.

Out of Lurianic kabbalah grew a number of powerful ideas that rabbis speak about today. For example, the kabbalah teaches that we live in four worlds, each world encompassed in the next higher world like Russian nested dolls. Tied to these four worlds is the four levels of the soul. The lowest of the four worlds is *Olam HaAsiya*, literally the world of action. Here the soul is called *nefesh*; it is the lowest level of consciousness. The next higher world is *Olam HaYitzirah*, literally the world of formation. Here the soul is called *ruach*, the emotional soul. The next higher world is *Olam HaBeriah*, literally the world of creation. Here the soul is called *neshama*, literally the breath of God. Other animals have a *ruach*, but only humans have a *neshama*. I like to call this the world of reflection, for only humans have a soul able to reflect on other souls.

The highest level is *Olam HaAtzilut*, the world of emanation. The word *etzel* literally means "next to," as if in this world everything is next to everything else. Everything touches. Think about the entanglement we spoke about it the previous chapter, where objects separated across space touch one another. Everything is entangled. The soul in this world is called *chaya*. It is in rare moments that we humans can reach this high level of insight. Mystics speak about a highest level of the soul called *yehidah*, the soul before it is born, still in the spiritual world. I wrote my book *The Kabbalah of Love: The Story of a Soul* about these four kabbalistic worlds and the various levels of the soul. The book asks the question, what does it mean to love someone in each of these four levels?

What about the masculine and the feminine in Lurianic kabbalah? I am aware that any discussion of gender in this age of political correctness can lead to severe criticism. But it is impossible to take kabbalah seriously without discussing gender. Luria introduced a brilliant insight regarding this notion of masculine and feminine aspects of reality—circles (*igullim*) and straightness (*yosher*). Scholar of kabbalah Mordecai Pachter in his essay "Circles and Straightness"[16] describes the fundamental idea:

> Rabbi Hayyim Vital [interpreter of Luria's work] presents the pair of concepts, "circles" and "lines" ("straightness") for the first time, representing two different aspects of the nature of the *sefirot*. In this sense, it is an attempt to resolve a problem arising from classic Kabbalistic sources, where descriptions of the *sefirot* as concentric circles intermingle with others of a linear hierarchic order, without adequate explanation for the inconsistency or even contradictions between the two. Vital's solution is that "Both are the living word of God," not contradictory descriptions, but compatible ones, since they represent two aspects of one nature, two formal aspects for conceptualizing the divine *sefirot*.[17]

The lines, or the straightness, are identified with the masculine aspects of reality; the circles are identified with the feminine aspects of reality. "Indeed the interaction between straightness and circles is none other than a sexual relationship in which straightness is identified with the male and circles with the female, i.e. the *sefirah* Yesod and the *sefirah* Malkhut."[18]

Why lines and circles? Think back to an earlier chapter in this book when we spoke of evolution. At that time we quoted how Rabbi Abraham Isaac Kook understood evolution in terms of kabbalah. The masculine aspects of reality, symbolized by lines, are those that break forth into new areas, evolve, and lead to the emergence of new ways. Without them the

16. This is an English translation of Pachter, *Igullim veYosher*.

17. Pachter, *Roots*, 131.

18. Pachter, *Roots*, 143.

world cannot move forward. Lines are necessary for emergence to take place. But lines can also lead to randomness and chaos. There must be a force that conserves the past, that protects old habits, and that prevents total randomness from overtaking reality. The circles represent the conservative tendency in the world.

The circles are a conserving force. They represent old ways. They protect against total chaos. The masculine tendencies are those that break outside of themselves to create new realities. Remember the previous comparison to sperm. But this creativity can burst forth out of control. The feminine tendencies are those that limit creativity, form protective walls. They are compared to the womb. Without this protective wall, chaos can reign. When the universe is out of balance, chaos is the result. When the universe is back in balance, the creative tendencies are balanced with the protective tendencies.

Allow me to turn for a moment to my own PhD dissertation. The goal of my dissertation was to look at these Jewish mystical ideas through the lens of Whitehead's process philosophy. In looking at circles and straightness, I found one of the most fascinating insights of my dissertation. Remember that Whitehead's world is made up of individual moments of consciousness that prehend other moments of consciousness and move forward creatively. That is why it is called process philosophy.

Whitehead does not speak of masculine and feminine in his description of actual entities. But he does speak of the potential for some entities to break forth in new directions, moving creatively forward, but sometimes as a result, descending into chaos. In fact, his concern about preventing chaos is an important part of his vision. Each actual entity or occasion has freedom and autonomy to go in whatever direction it chooses. It has the vision of the lure—God's superject nature. But it also has the freedom to go off in any direction. And sometimes that direction leads to chaos. Whitehead writes about the balance between order and chaos. He claims that the advance into creativity entails the threat of chaos. Nonetheless, without such an advance there can be no progress.

Whitehead is not the easiest writer to comprehend. But it is worth quoting him on this subject:

> Thus, if there is to be progress beyond limited ideals, the course
> of history by way of escape must venture along the borders of
> chaos in its substitution of higher for lower types of order. The
> immanence of God gives reason for the belief that pure chaos
> is intrinsically impossible. At the other end of the scale, the im-
> mensity of the world negatives the belief that any state of order

can be so established that beyond it there can be no progress. The belief in a final order, popular in religious and philosophic thought, seems to be due to the prevalent fallacy that all types of seriality necessarily involve terminal instances. It follows that Tennyson's phrase "one far off divine event to which the whole creation moves"[19] presents a fallacious conception of the universe.[20]

Whitehead, whose entire metaphysics is built around evolution and process, teaches that without the bursting forth and creativity of individual entities there can be no such evolution and no progress. The quote from Tennyson shows that there is no final end with which this progress will come to a halt. Evolution and process will continue. On the other hand, without the conserving qualities to sustain order, the process can lose control and chaos can reign. Balance is necessary in the evolution of the individual entities.

Finally, Whitehead speaks of the human need to find such a balance between preserving the past and moving creatively into the future. He writes: "The world is faced by the paradox that, at least in the higher actualities, it craves for novelty and yet is haunted by terror at the loss of the past, with its familiarities and its loved ones."[21] I often find myself thinking of Whitehead as I try to lead my congregation, on one hand moving creatively forward but on the other hand, respecting the conservative tendencies of the past. Too much innovation and anarchy can reign, where the links to the past have been broken. Too much conservation and creativity if lost, the synagogue becoming a museum to the past. Every decent rabbi must constantly walk this tightrope suggested by Whitehead.

Therefore, in both the *Zohar* and Whitehead, we begin to see an image of process in the universe. Process is the balance of two forces symbolized in kabbalistic thought by the masculine and the feminine, lines and circles. According to this interpretation, the masculine aspect of reality, the line, is what allows the universe to move forward, forming new types and allowing emergence to take place. But the masculine aspect out of control can lead to chaos and a breakdown of reality. According to this interpretation, the feminine aspect of reality, the circle, holds the masculine aspect in check, conserving old ways and maintaining old habits. But the feminine devoid of the masculine will become stuck in a repetitive pattern, with no hope

19. From Alfred Lord Tennyson's 1849 poem "In Memoriam." The closing stanza is: "That God, which ever lives and loves, One God, one law, one element, And one far-off divine event, To which the whole creation moves." The last three lines are inscribed in the main reading room of the Library of Congress.

20. Whitehead, *Process and Reality*, 111.

21. Whitehead, *Process and Reality*, 516.

for progress and no room for renewal. Only when the masculine and the feminine are brought into balance can progress be made. And returning to *Zohar*'s language, this will only happen when the moon and the sun are back in balance.

CONCLUSION

In the End, What Is Consciousness?

A group of students was discussing God with their Rebbe. One of them asked, "Rebbe, how far are we from God?" The Rebbe responded, "As far as east is from west." "That far," said the student. "At the equator that is over 12,000 miles." "That far," said the Rebbe. Then a second student asked the Rebbe, "Rebbe, how far are we from God?" The Rebbe responded, "As far as east is from west." "That close," said the student. "I can be facing east, turn around, and face west." "That close," said the Rebbe.

We have now studied three very different creation stories and the various implications of their insights. The first creation story saw God creating a world outside God's very self. The second creation story saw preexistent matter and God within that matter, moving it from chaos to order. The third creation story saw God as making an empty space within God's self and emanating a world within that self. One of my students asked if I would draw Venn diagrams of these three creation stories. Perhaps this would make them easier to picture:

Venn Diagrams For Three Creation Stories

Creation Story #1

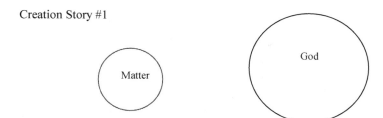

God creates matter (the universe) outside God's self.

Creation Story #2

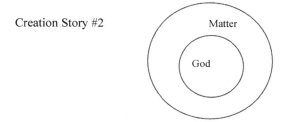

God is the force in matter (the universe) that goes from chaos to order.

Creation Story #3

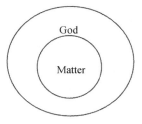

God makes a space within God's self for matter (the universe) to appear.

The first creation story was the view of classical theism, the view of the majority of religious Jews, Christians, and Muslims in the world. It is the view I learned at the Jewish Theological Seminary and the view I taught through the first several decades of my career. It was a dualist vision of reality—matter and mind or body and soul. An all-powerful God created the universe from nothing, made humans out of mere matter, and breathed a soul of life into those humans. When we die our bodies will return to the dust but our souls, the breath of God, will return to God. There we may spend eternity, hopefully in *Gan Eden*—the Garden of Eden. There our bodies may also be returned to us, either through resurrection of our same bodies or reincarnation into new bodies. God is transcendent, beyond this world, like the first student in the story who sees east and west as thousands of miles away.

We learned that the biggest problem with this particular approach is the interplay between body and soul. How can a nonmaterial substance affect a material substance, and how can a material substance affect a nonmaterial substance? This is the problem that has caused most modern scientists and philosophers to reject substance dualism. While we were exploring classical theism, we also explored three issues at the heart of religious belief. Does God perform miracles by changing the laws of nature, or is a miracle simply a way of looking at an entirely natural event? Why would a perfectly good God create a world so seemingly filled with evil, or is the evil illusionary? Does evil fulfill some kind of divine purpose? Is God the source of ethics, defining what is good and what is evil, or do ethics have some kind of existence beyond God? In exploring these issues, we confronted the problems of philosophical dualism.

Our second creation story assumed a totally material world. God is simply the force within nature that causes order to arise out of chaos, making for greater and greater complexity. But if God acts on matter to move it in the direction of complexity, does this not defy the fundamental laws of thermodynamics? The first law teaches that energy cannot be added to a closed system, so how does God act on the world? The second law is even more problematic, teaching that in a closed system matter moves from organization to chaos. How could chaos moving to order be reconciled with the laws of entropy?

We viewed two other issues central to the materialist view of the world. Is evolution a totally blind process, based on random chance and totally directionless? Or is there some underlying direction that serves as the ultimate goal of evolution? But if there is such a goal, are we not introducing Aristotle's final causation into the world, an idea that philosophers and scientists have rejected since the Renaissance? The more difficult question is, how do we account for mind or consciousness in such a material world?

Is mind a mere epiphenomenon, is it a function, or to paraphrase Thomas Nagel, is there something that it is like to be conscious? Could we build a computer or robot with consciousness, or is that simply the dream of science fiction writers?

Our third creation story was built on idealism, the fact that mind is the ultimate reality. Matter exists in the fact that it is perceived by a mind, to quote the famous idealist George Berkeley. We looked at idealism in the East, and how Hinduism, Buddhism, and Daoism see mind as the ultimate reality. We also looked at idealism in the West, exploring Plotinus's Neoplatonism and various forms of mysticism. We also looked at idealistic philosophy among many philosophers since the Enlightenment, including Kant, Hegel, and Whitehead. And we asked the question that lurked in the background of ancient animism, modern romanticism, and contemporary deep ecology: Is nature somehow alive with spirit? If so, does nature have rights?

We spoke of Kant's turn to the subject, and spoke about its influence in physics since the beginning of the twentieth century. Both Einstein's theory of relativity and quantum theory are built on the centrality of the observer. In fact, in quantum theory it is observation by a conscious observer that causes the collapse of the Schrodinger equation. We spoke about how difficult it is to pin down light, and suggested that perhaps light is simply a metaphor for mind. Finally, we explored mysticism in general and, in particular, the kabbalah of the *Zohar* and Isaac Luria. Both are based on the idea of emanation of God, or light, or mind, into the world. Such a God is immanent in the world, like the second student in the story above, who sees east and west as next to each other. We learned the centrality of humanity in unleashing the divine sparks, and in bringing together the masculine and the feminine, the sun and the moon, the lines and the circles.

What underlines this entire book is role of consciousness, mind, spirit, soul, or subjectivity in the universe. David Chalmers called this the hard problem of consciousness. For dualists, mind and matter are both creations of God. But if they are two separate substances, how can they interact with one another? For materialists, there is only matter. But how can mind emerge from a world made of mere stuff? For idealists, mind is the ultimate reality. But then what is matter, and why do we seem to live in a world made of matter? I am struggling to find an answer to all these questions. But I know that until we tackle the problem of mind or consciousness, we cannot begin to understand what it means to live in the universe.

Consciousness as a Field

Allow me to offer one possible solution. Many physicists today say that matter is not the ultimate building block of the universe. According to Sean Carroll, Caltech theoretical physicist, author of numerous books, and professor for The Teaching Company of the course on "The Higgs Boson," the universe is made of fields. Fields are spread out and fill space. Today we know that gravitational attraction is a field, as is electromagnetism. Einstein's general relativity is based on difficult field equations. Fields give us a value for every point in space. If everything is a field, then what is a particle? According to Carroll, particles are simply disturbances of these fields. Carroll claims that such excitations of fields are simply like waves in the ocean. When two particles interact, it is actually two fields interacting, perhaps creating a third field whose disturbance is a third particle.[1]

David Chalmers has already claimed that consciousness is a fundamental fact of the universe. What if consciousness is simply a field filling all space-time? We have already used the metaphor of waves in the ocean, the same metaphor Carroll uses for particles in a field. What if consciousness is a field, which manifests itself in individual particles, but they never stop being part of the greater field? That is why we can have entanglement of particles separated by a great distance, because separate particles are part of the one field. What if our individual consciousness was also a manifestation of this universal consciousness, similar to *Atman* is *Brahman*? What if Whitehead is right and the fundamental building blocks of reality are moments of consciousness, each one prehending every other one? What if the kabbalists are right when they said that our individual souls are called *yehidah*, from a Hebrew root meaning "connected"? Every soul is connected to every other soul. Such an image of universal consciousness would certainly fit the vision that Jews have been proclaiming twice a day, that God is One. Everything is One, part of the great field, the one universal consciousness.

Does this answer the question of the role of consciousness in the universe? If mind is a field and my individual consciousness is a disturbance in that field, then when I die my consciousness becomes part of something greater than myself. Returning to the oft-used metaphor, our minds are like waves in the ocean. Perhaps death is like that moment the wave nears the shore. When we die, our individual consciousness may exist for a while, a time when we are reunited with loved ones. But eventually our individual consciousness will fade into the one consciousness, which is the universe. We are all part of the universal mind. In the end, we are all part of the One,

1. Jepsen, "Real Talk."

the great unity of everything. That is a view of consciousness in keeping with my sense, as a rabbi, of what is reality.

Bibliography

Aquinas, Thomas. *Summa Theologica: First Complete American Edition in Three Volumes.* Translated by Fathers of the English Dominican Province, Vol. 1. New York: Benziger Brothers, 1947.

Aristotle. *Aristotle's Metaphysics.* Translated by Hippocrates George Apostle. Bloomington: Indiana University Press, 1966.

Asimov, Isaac. "The Last Question." In *Nine Tomorrows: Tales of the Near Future.* New York: Doubleday, 1959.

Bacon, Francis. *Novum Organon,* in *The Philosophical Works of Francis Bacon.* Edited by John M. Robertson. London: Routledge and Sons, 1905.

Berger, Peter. *The Sacred Canopy: Elements of a Sociological Theory.* Garden City, NY: Doubleday, 1969.

Berger, Peter L., and Thomas Luckmann. *The Social Construction of Reality.* New York: Random House, 1966.

Berman, Morris. *The Reenchantment of the World.* Ithaca, NY: Cornell University Press, 1981.

Cahill, Thomas. *The Gifts of the Jews.* New York: Nan A. Talese/Anchor, 1998.

Carroll, Sean. *The Higgs Boson and Beyond.* Chantilly, VA: Teaching Company Course, 2015.

Carson, Rachel. *Silent Spring.* New York: Houghton Mifflin, 1962.

Chalmers, David. *The Conscious Mind: In Search of a Fundamental Theory.* New York: Oxford University Press, 1996.

Crick, Frances. *The Astonishing Hypothesis: The Scientific Search for the Soul.* New York: Touchstone Books, 1994.

Dawkins, Richard. *The Blind Watchmaker.* New York: Norton, 1986.

Dennett, Daniel C. *Consciousness Explained.* Boston: Back Bay, 1991.

Doniger, Wendy, ed. *The Norton Anthology of World Religions.* New York: Norton, 2015.

Easlea, Brian. *Witch Hunting, Magic, and the New Philosophy: An Introduction to Debates of the Scientific Revolution, 1450–1750.* Sussex: Harvester, 1980.

Gleiser, Marcelo. *The Tear at the Edge of Creation: A Radical New Vision for Life in an Imperfect Universe.* New York: Free Press, 2010.

Gold, Michael. "A Whiteheadian Interpretation of the Zoharic Creation Story." PhD diss., Florida Atlantic University, 2016.

——. "Let There Be Light: An Exploration of Science and Religion." *Jewish Spectator* (Spring 2000).

——. *The Kabbalah of Love: The Story of a Soul.* Charleston, SC: Booksurge, 2008.

Graber, David M. "Mother Nature as a Hothouse Flower." Review of *The End of Nature*, by Bill McGibben. *Los Angeles Times* (October 22, 1989). http://articles.latimes. com/1989-10-22/books/bk-726_1_bill-mckibben.

Green, Arthur. "*Shekhinah*, the Virgin Mary, and the Song of Songs: Reflections on a Kabbalistic Symbol in Its Historical Context." *Association for Jewish Studies Review* 26 (2002) 1–52.

Greenberg, Sidney, and Jonathan D. Levine, eds. *Siddur Hadash*. New York: Media Judaica, 2007.

Greenblatt, Stephen. *The Swerve: How the World Became Modern*. New York: Norton, 2011.

Griffin, David Ray. *Reenchantment Without Supernaturalism*. Ithaca, NY: Cornell University Press, 2001.

Harmon, William, and Elisabet Sahtouris. *Biology Revisioned*. Berkeley, CA: North Atlantic, 1998.

Harris, Sam. *The Moral Landscape: How Science Can Determine Human Values*. New York: Free Press, 2010.

Hobbes, Thomas. *Leviathan or The Matter, Forme and Power of a Common-wealth Ecclesiasticall and Civil*. Edited by Rod Hay, n.d. First published 1651. https:// socialsciences.mcmaster.ca/econ/ugcm/3ll3/hobbes/Leviathan.pdf, p. 78.

Hofstadter, Douglas R. *Gödel, Escher, Bach: An Eternal Golden Braid*. New York: Basic, 1979.

Hume, David. *Dialogues Concerning Natural Religion*. Edited by Jonathan Bennett. Early Modern Texts, 2017 (originally published 1779). http://www.earlymoderntexts. com/assets/pdfs/hume1779.pdf.

————. *Enquiry Concerning Human Understanding*. "On Miracles." Edited by Jonathan Bennett. Early Modern Texts, 2017 (originally published 1748). http://www. earlymoderntexts.com/assets/pdfs/hume1748.pdf.

James, William. "Does Consciousness Exist?" *Journal of Philosophy, Psychology, and Scientific Method* 1 (September 1, 1904) 477–91.

Jepsen, Kathryn. "Real Talk: Everything Is Made of Fields." *Symmetry* (July 18, 2013). https://www.symmetrymagazine.org/article/july-2013/real-talk-everything-is-made-of-fields.

Jonas, Hans. *Mortality and Morality: A Search for the Good after Auschwitz*. Edited by Lawrence Vogel. Evanston, IL: Northwestern University Press, 1996.

————. *The Gnostic Religion: The Message of the Alien God and the Beginnings of Christianity*. Boston: Beacon, 2001.

Jones, Charles P. *Introduction to the Study of Religion*. Chantilly, VA: Teaching Company Course, 2007.

Kapstein, Matthew. *The Presence of Light*. Chicago: University of Chicago Press, 2004.

Kook, Abraham Isaac. *Orot HaKodesh*. Edited by David Cohen. Jerusalem: Mossad HaRav Kook, 1963–1964 (Vol. 1–3), 1990 (Vol. 4).

Kuhn, Thomas S. *The Structure of Scientific Revolutions*. Chicago: University of Chicago Press, 1962.

Kushner, Harold. *When Bad Things Happen to Good People*. New York: Random House, 1981.

Lucas, J. R. "Minds, Machines, and Gödel. *Philosophy* 36 (April—July 1961) 112–127.

Matt, Daniel. *"Ayin:* The Concept of Nothingness in Jewish Mysticism." *Essential Papers on Kabbalah.* Edited by Lawrence Fine, 67–108. New York: New York University Press, 2000.

———. *God and the Big Bang: Discovering Harmony Between Science and Spirituality.* Woodstock, VT: Jewish Lights, 1996.

———. *The Essential Kabbalah.* San Francisco: Harper, 1995.

———. *The Zohar = [Sefer Ha-Zohar] 11 Vols.* Pritzker ed. Stanford, CA: Stanford University Press, 2004–2017.

Mittleman, Alan L. *Human Nature and Jewish Thought: Judaism's Case for Why Persons Matter.* Princeton, NJ: Princeton University Press, 2015.

Nagel, Ernest, and James R. Neuman. *Gödel's Proof.* New York: New York University Press, 2001.

Nagel, Thomas. "What Is It Like to Be a Bat?" *The Philosophical Review* 83 (October 1974) 435–50.

Nicholson, Reynold A. Nicholson. *The Mystics of Islam.* London: Routledge, Kegan Paul, 1914. Retrieved from http://www.sacred-texts.com/isl/moi/moi.htm.

Orgel, Leslie E. "The Origin of Life on Earth." *Scientific American* 271 (October 1994) 76–83.

Pachter, Mordechai. "Igullim veYosher—LeToldoteha shel Idea." *Daat* 18 (1987) 59–110.

———. *Roots of Faith and Devequt: Studies in the History of Kabbalistic Ideas,* 10 Vol. Los Angeles: Cherub, 2004.

Paley, William. *Natural Theology.* New York: American Tract Society, 1881.

Penrose, Roger. *The Emperor's New Mind: Concerning Computers, Minds, and the Laws of Physics.* Oxford: Oxford University Press, 1989.

Philo. "On the Cherubim." In *3 Jewish Philosophers.* Edited by Hans Lewy. New Milford, CT: Toby, 2006.

Plantinga, Alfred. *Where the Conflict Really Lies: Science, Religion, and Naturalism.* Oxford: Oxford University Press, 2011.

Plato. *Dialogues of Plato.* Translated by Benjamin Jowett. New York: Simon and Schuster Paperbacks, 2010.

Plotinus. *The Enneads.* Edited by Stephen MacKenna. London: Faber, 1969.

Prigogine, Ilya, and Isabelle Stengers. *Order Out of Chaos: Man's Dialogue with Nature.* New York: Bantam, 1984.

Singer, Peter. *Animal Liberation.* New York: HarperCollins, 1975.

Sommers, Tamler. "Darrow and Determinism: Giving Up Ultimate Responsibility." Naturalism.com (September 2004). http:// http://www.naturalism.org/ philosophy/free-will/darrow-and-determinism.

Spinoza, Benedict de. *A Theologico-Political Treatise.* Translated by R. H. M. Elwes. New York: Dover, 1951.

Teilhard de Chardin, Pierre. *Building the Earth and The Psychological Conditions of Human Unification.* New York: Avon (Discus Edition), 1969.

———. *The Phenomenon of Man.* New York: Harper & Row, 1975.

Wald, George. "Life and Mind in the Universe." *Quantum Chemistry* (March 12, 1984). Quoted in Harmon and Sahtouris.

Weber, Max. *Max Weber's "Science as a Vocation."* Translated by Michael John; edited by Peter Lassman and Irving Velody. London: Oxford University Press, 1989.

Weinberg, Steven. *The First Three Minutes: A Modern View of the Origin of the Universe.* Updated. New York: Basic Books, 1993.

White, Ethan Doyle. *Wicca: History, Belief, and Community in Modern Pagan Witchcraft.* Eastbourne, UK: Sussex Academic Press, 2016.

White, Lynn, Jr. "The Historical Roots of Our Ecological Crisis." *Science* 155 (March 10, 1967) 1203–1207.

Whitehead, Alfred North. *Process and Reality.* Edited by David Ray Griffin and Donald W. Sherburne. New York: Free Press, 1978.

Wu, Laurence. "Light and Mirror: Two Mystic Metaphors of Mind." *The Philosophy Forum* 14 (1974) 145–160.

Yates, Frances Amelia. *Giordano Bruno and the Hermetic Tradition.* Chicago: University of Chicago Press, 1964.

Zajonc, Arthur. *Catching the Light: The Entwined History of Light and Mind.* New York: Oxford University Press, 1995.

Index

Made in the USA
Columbia, SC
08 March 2021